About the Author:

Dr Michael Paraskos was born in Leeds in the north of England, and he studied at the School of Fine Art
of the University of Leeds. Later he gained his doctorate, researching the aesthetic theories
of Herbert Read, at the University of Nottingham.

He was previously Head of Art History for Fine Art at the University of Hull,
and has been Henry Moore Fellow in Sculpture Studies at the University of Leeds
and Henry Moore Institute. He was Director of the Cyprus College of Art and the Cornaro Institute,
and he has lectured on art at universities and other institutions around the world, including the
University of Cambridge, University of Oxford, University of Nicosia, the American University of Beirut,
University of Graz, National College of Art and Design in Dublin, Tate Britain, the Whitechapel
and the Academie Minerva, to name but a few.

He is a contributor to newspapers, magazines, radio and television, the BBC, *The Spectator, The Epoch Times*
and *The British Art Journal,* and academic journals including *The Art Book, The Sculpture Journal* and *The Journal of
the History of Education* amongst others. He is the founder and lead organiser
of the annual conference *Othello's Island.*

His first job, however, was as an apprentice butcher.
Despite his Grandfather being a Master Butcher, this was a short lived experience
that turned Michael into a life long vegetarian.

His website is at http://www.michaelparaskos.net

ISBN: 978-09929247-2-0

First published by The **Orage** Press
16A Heaton Road
Mitcham
Surrey
CR4 2BU
England

For Stass

Herbert Read:
Art and Idealism

INTRODUCTION

Herbert Read was one of the most influential art and literary theorists of modernism active in the first half of the twentieth century. He is frequently credited with bringing modern art and modernism to a wide public and was dubbed by friends and foes alike the 'Pope of Modern Art.'[1] As a broadcaster on the BBC and a prolific writer Read was a well known public figure, but his understanding of art, literature and society was built on sometimes recondite forms of Continental Philosophy, particularly idealist philosophy, albeit at the point where idealist philosophy and romantic ideology meet. That he was able to turn these into a theory of culture admired not only by artists,

---

1 See Ian Chilvers, *The Oxford Dictionary of Art* (Oxford: Oxford University Press, 2004) 578

writers and political activists but the wider public is a measure of his skill as a thinker and writer.

In what was effectively a lifelong project, Read's aim was little short of extraordinary. Through art he sought to ameliorate what he saw as the suffering of the human soul after its fracture at the hands of modern society and culture. As well as philosophy, his method drew a great deal on contemporary theories of psychoanalysis, with Read characterising the artist almost as a kind of psychotherapist for society. Read's project had a goal, the reintegration of the self into something whole again, but his method was also integrationist, and it led him to seek to combine often competing and sometimes contradictory theories of society and culture, philosophy and psychotherapy.

The ability to contemplate and accept contradiction, Read believed, was a key element in human life, with art holding a position in human culture as the reconciler of these differences. Speaking on this in 1958 Read cited the psychotherapist Carl Gustav Jung, claiming that for Jung the human condition is a series of antithetical positions. These needed balancing out and for Read the balance was possible through a process he termed the 'will to integration.'[2]

We will follow this line of thought in more detail later in this book, but it is worth noting briefly how difficult proposing the notion of reconciling opposites was for Read. Amongst his artist friends Read found little appetite to even contemplate that there might be a kind of third way between the polar positions of one side and the other, to the extent that Read lamented he sometimes felt he was like, 'a circus rider with his feet planted astride two horses.'[3]

This difficulty was not confined to Read's friends in the art world. In his political activism one of the key tenets of Read's developing theory, an integration of idealist philosophy with anarchist theory, was also problematic. In light of the fulsome diatribe against philosophical idealism by one of the

2 Herbert Read, 'The Creative Nature of Humanism', in *Eranos Jahrbuch,* vol. XXVI, 1957, 332-4.

3 Herbert Read, 'A Nest of Gentle Artists', *Apollo,* vol. LXXVI, no. 7, 1962, reproduced in Benedict Read and David Thistlewood, *Herbert Read: A British Vision of World Art* (London: Lund Humphries, 1992) 60

leading figures in early anarchist thought, Mikhail Bakunin, it was arguably perverse for Read to even suggest anarchism and idealist philosophy might be natural bedfellows. According to Bakunin the metaphysical abstractions of idealism, divorced from material reality, lead to unverifiable ideas such as God, and ultimately stemming from these the 'consecration of slavery'.[4] Even before he had embraced anarchism overtly, Read too had a dislike of this dematerialist aspect of idealism, writing in 1933: 'I have never been able to believe that the idealistic conception of art... is worth the time that would be involved in mastering its mysteries.' All that romanticist discussion of imagination and fancy, form and idea, he suggested, is rarely relevant to the objective reality of art.[5]

Yet, later in life, once he had fully embraced political anarchism, Read came to believe there were similarities. Indeed, one of the ways we can conceptualise the mature work of Read

4 Mikhail Bakunin, *Political Philosophy: Scientific Anarchism,* ed. G.P. Maximoff (London: Free Press of Glencoe, 1984) 146

5 Herbert Read, *Art Now* (London: Faber and Faber, 1933) 35-9

is to see it as an attempt to reconcile the material, or we might say physical, philosophy of anarchism with the seemingly immaterial, or metaphysical, philosophy of idealism. It was an attempt that was to be blazoned in the very titles of Read's later writings on art and literature, including *Icon and Idea, The Forms of Things Unknown* and *Reason and Romanticism*. In each case there was a dualism that was to become core to Read's understanding of both art and life.

Perhaps the best starting point to achieve an understanding of Read's attempt to unify anarchism and idealism is to recognise the emphasis both place on the individual mind. For most anarchists the human presence in the world should be as comfortable, pleasant and fulfilling as possible. Most hypothesised anarchist communities are seen as a means to ensure comfort, pleasure and fulfilment for all people based on a belief that this is how human society would exist naturally if it was not warped by unnatural phenomena, such as private property, self-appointed elites and institutional religion. Through this warping a small number of people obtain comfort, pleasure and fulfilment at the expense of the vast majority. In proposing its radical alternative anarchism differs from classic Marxism by refusing to predetermine what makes life comfortable, pleasant and fulfilling. Anarchism recognises individuals have different concepts of comfort, pleasure and fulfilment, and so the lover of extreme sports might well find the life of a bookish lover of poetry frustratingly dull, and vice versa. But anarchism also recognises that desires change over surprisingly short spaces of time, so that the lover of extreme sports today might be a lover of poetry tomorrow. For this reason any rigid system, such as a permanent institution or set of rules that ossifies needs and desires, is an inorganic imposition on life that risks entrapping individuals in a fixed state, resulting in frustration and alienation. It is the organic reality of individual human beings that is understood by anarchists to be the nature of humanity.

This was nicely summed up by Read himself when he wrote: 'I find it hard to accept any ontology or theory of life which insists on a single and exclusive reaction to experience.'[6] In accepting infinitely multiple reactions to experience what Read and other anarchists sought to do was empower the individual to react not as an external force says they should react, but as they want and need to react. Today I might want and need to climb a mountain, but tomorrow I might want and need to read Shelley, and being human it is my nature to have different needs in reaction to different experiences at different times.

In prioritising the individual in this way anarchism does indeed seem to have some affinities with philosophical idealism. Idealism places an emphasis on the human mind over the external appearance of the world. Defining it Immanuel Kant said idealism was the belief that: 'we can never be certain whether all of our putative outer experience is not mere imagining.'[7] One of the most well known of the idealists, George

6 Herbert Read, *The Philosophy of Modern Art* (London: Faber and Faber, 1952), 97

7 Immanuel Kant, *Notes and Fragments,* ed. Paul Guyer, trans. by Curtis Bowman, Paul Guyer, and Frederick Rauscher, (Cambridge: Cambridge University Press, 2005) 361

Berkeley had a similar definition to the extent he is frequently characterised as claiming that existence is all in the mind. This doctrine is often summarised with the Latin tag, *Esse est percipi*, or *To be is to be perceived*.[8] With both Kant and Berkeley what we have is a definition of idealism in which reality, at least as it is known to the human mind, is seen as a product of the human mind. This in turn implies the possibility that an individual mind might reconstruct reality according to its own desires and imaginings. In this idealism has is a clear correspondence with the individualistic elements of romanticism, which makes aspects of idealism and romanticism synonymous. But this point can also be mapped onto a core anarchist belief that individual minds freed from the shackles imposed on them by socially dominant elites would be free to reconstruct society as each individual chose.

The process of making a world in a painting or other work of art seems a useful metaphor for all of this, or even a

8 See Georges Dicker, *Berkeley's Idealism: A Critical Examination* (Oxford: Oxford University Press, 2011) 3

theoretical model, as the artist can be viewed as an individual freed from the conventions of our reality to create a new reality on his or her canvas. This can be extended across the arts into poetry, novels, plays, films and so on, but it is also occasionally manifest in the political discourse. In the proto-anarchist writings of Charles Fourier, for example, Fourier suggested a post-revolutionary world should be revolutionarily different to a pre-revolutionary world.[9] Because of this a post-revolutionary world, freed of the partiality of pre-existing social structures, would be so unlike our world that even the reality of nature might be different. Dangerous tigers and crocodiles might turn into helpful anti-tigers and anti-crocodiles, Fourier claimed, while the briny sea might turn into something like lemonade.[10] There is a debate whether Fourier meant these suggestions literally, but the point he makes about radicalism is a

9 I discuss this in more detail in Michael Paraskos, 'What would an anarchist Rembrandt look like?' originally delivered at the Anarchist Studies Network Annual Conference at the University of Loughborough, September 2012, reproduced in *Sanat Dünyamız*, no. 131, November 2012, 22f

10 Charles Fourier, *Oeuvres Complètes, v*ol. IV, 2nd ed. (Paris, 1841) 254f

sound one. It should indeed propose something radically different to our current existence. Combining this with idealism would therefore suggest that individual thought freed by revolutionary action would in effect lead to an individual construction of a new reality.

Despite this, anarchism has often been loathe to embrace idealism. Pierre-Joseph Proudhon was particularly scathing of philosophical idealism, and all forms of metaphysics, arguing instead for a materialist philosophy that could be of use in society. Like the beliefs of the religious miracle worker or the fairground somnambulist, 'idealism, whether subjective, objective or absolute, and all the practices of the great work of alchemy, has never produced for indigent humanity an ounce of bread, has created neither shoes, not hats, nor shirts; so it will not have added an iota to knowledge.'[11] As Alex Prichard points out, in one of the few sustained studies to date dealing with the question of anarchism and philosophical idealism, for Proudhon,

---

11 Pierre-Joseph Proudhon, 'That metaphysics is within the province of primary instruction', in *Justice in the Revolution and in the Church,* vol. 1 (1858) § v.

'The flaw of idealism was to confuse the ego with the ultimate source of truth, to de-link the individual from social context.'[12]

Here Read faced a conundrum. Both anarchism and idealism shared a belief in the primacy of the individual, but apparently for anarchism that individual was rooted in a material and social reality, whereas for idealism the individual somehow had the potential to be a kind of supra-social being, akin to Friedrich Nietzsche's superman. That is to say a being able to transcend their own social context. This is a gross simplification of course, as both idealism and anarchism are terms that seek to label very diverse philosophies and phenomena, not all of which would take these characterisations.[13] But unless we recognise that Read's anarchism was infused with a strong dose of philosophical idealism, much of it sourced from his early encounter with the

12 Alex Prichard, Justice, *Order and Anarchy: The international political theory of Pierre-Joseph* Proudhon (London: Routledge, 2013) 67

13 See Karl Ameriks (ed.), *The Cambridge Companion to German Idealism* (Cambridge: Cambridge University Press, 2000) 7-10.

writings of Nietzsche,[14] it is difficult to understand his beliefs about art and politics.

Read's solution was to embrace a form of romantic idealism in which the inner reality of the self was hybridised (or more accurately synthesised) with the outer experience of the material world to form what we understand to be reality. Consequently, for Read, every human was a dialectical being, a view derived partly from his interest in psychoanalysis, so that the introvert and the extrovert, the inner self and the outer personality, hypothesised by Jung, existed in a dialectical tension within and around each of us. Read made this point more precisely by correlating Jung's dialectics of internal-external and introvert-extrovert to the historic division between classicism and romanticism, quoting at one point André Gide's words: 'It is important to remember that the struggle between classicism and romanticism also exists inside each mind.'[15]

14 See Tom Steele, *Alfred Orage and the Leeds Arts Club 1893-1923* (Mitcham: Orage Press, 2009) 218f

15 Herbert Read 'Psycho-analysis and the Critic', in *The Criterion*, vol.3, no.10, 1925, 221

Perhaps then there is a question worth raising whether it is possible also to map these categories onto anarchism and idealism themselves, with the supra-social individual of Nietzsche's idealism resembling the introvert and the social individual of Proudhon's anarchism resembling the extrovert. It was through partial recourse to the theories of figures such as Jung and Gide, but also manifestations of romantic cultural theory stemming from the likes of the Victorian art critic John Ruskin and Nietzsche,[16] that Read attempted to transcend the apparent dislike of anarchism for idealism, using an integrationist theory of art and society which attempted to undermine the longstanding historic either-or nature of the debate.

This seems to give us a theory for understanding Read's anarchist dialectics. From a starting point in Proudhon's materialist anarchism, Read embraced philosophical idealism and sought a unification of the two through Jungian psychology. If

---

16 For contextual study on whether Nietzsche should be considered a romantic philosopher, which would be to go against his own wishes, see Caroline Joan ("Kay") S. Picart, 'Nietzsche as Masked Romantic', in *The Journal of Aesthetics and Art Criticism,* vol. 55, no. 3, Summer, 1997, 273f

this has a flaw as a theory it is that it has yet to take account of Proudhon's own dialectical engagement with idealism. As Prichard has shown, although Proudhon dismissed idealism his own anarchism was itself the product of dialectical interplay between the idealism of Kant and the scientific-materialism of Auguste Comte. Notably Proudhon had Jean-Jacques Rousseau to add romantic revolutionary fervour to his dialectical mix, much as Read had Nietzsche to do the same. Proudhon's anarchism thus acted, according to Prichard, as the solution to the problem of the binary division between thought and matter, and so by nomial extension, the binary division between romanticism and classicism.[17] This raises an interesting scenario by suggesting a possibly motivation for Read's embrace of anarchism was the solution it had already offered through Proudhon to this perceived problem.

Outside of politics, Read not only drew on the work of philosophers and psychotherapists, but cultural theorists,

17 Alex Prichard, *Justice, Order and Anarchy: The international political theory of Pierre-Joseph Proudhon* (London: Routledge, 2013) 67f and *passim*

including Charles Herford, Professor of English at Manchester's Victoria University. Herford shared Read's interest in German art and literature, including expressionism,[18] and seems to have led Read to understand romantic idealism not as the antithesis of classical materialism, but as the unifying factor in itself. If the dialectic was between inscape and outscape, to use Gerard Manley Hopkins's terminology, romantic idealism was not in Read's view a synonym for inscape, it was the solution to the problem of the division between the two. In this specific sense, Read's romantic idealism operated not unlike Proudhon's anarchism as a unifying factor.

What seems to emerge in Read is an apparent adherence to aspects of dialectical thinking that can fit, reasonably comfortably, under the label romantic idealism. But this was by no means a certain outcome. Read's thought processes were organic rather than dogmatic and because of this we see him change his mind, sometimes quite dramatically. It was a

18 See C.H. Herford, *The Post-War Mind of Germany And Other European Studies* (Oxford: Oxford University Press, 1927)

characteristic that led some critics to accuse him of being an inconsistent thinker, but it is perhaps more useful to characterise it as making Read a very human thinker.[19] It was not until the end of the 1920s that Read's own opposition to idealism began to wane. Initially this was due to a growing interest in the poetics of Samuel Taylor Coleridge, one of the most important early interlocutors between the German idealist tradition and British romantic art and literature.[20] Even then Read made a number of vehemently anti-idealist statements as late as 1933.[21] It was not until the late 1930s that Read came to be fully committed to romantic idealism, albeit in his own modified form,[22] and after the Second World War he

---

19 For example, Wyndham Lewis's well-known suggestion that Read was a supporter of any new art movement 'sometimes of the most contradictory kind'. Percy Wyndham Lewis, *The Demon of Progress in the Arts* (London: Methuen, 1954) 53

20 For example, see Read's use of Coleridge in *Wordsworth* (London: Jonathan Cape, 1930) 17 and passim.

21 For example see Herbert Read, *Art Now* (London: Faber and Faber, 1933) 35.

22 For examples see Herbert Read, *The True Voice of Feeling* (London: Faber and Faber, 1953) 15f; in *Essays in Literary Criticism* (London: Faber, 1951; 1969 reprint) 126 and passim, and in *Icon and Idea* (London: Faber, 1955), 39 and passim.

even embraced existentialism,[23] a philosophical movement with close affinities to some forms of idealism.[24] As we shall see, this embrace of idealism was contiguous with Read adopting anarchism as his political belief, to the point where he spoke publicly in 1948 on the similarities he saw between anarchism, idealism and existentialism.[25]

In his attempt to assimilate seemingly disparate ideas, Read was not engaged in an esoteric academic exercise. Rather he was attempting to formulate philosophy that would be drawn from lived experience and then re-applicable to life. His notion of modernity as a shattering of the previously coherent humanist philosophy of life was a familiar one even in his life time. But Read's refusal to accept either of the standard responses to that shattering experience was unusual and

23 Herbert Read, 'Coleridge as Critic', delivered as a lecture at Johns Hopkins University in 1948, reproduced in Herbert Read, *The True Voice of Feeling* (London: Faber and Faber, 1953), 180.

24 See Jon Stewart, *Idealism and Existentialism: Hegel and Nineteenth- and Twentieth-Century European Philosophy* (London: Continuum, 2010) 71f

25 This was in a lecture at Johns Hopkins University in 1948, later published by the anarchist Freedom Press as Herbert Read, *Existentialism, Marxism and Anarchism* (London: Freedom Press, 1949)

perhaps unique. There was no desire in Read to follow his friend T.S. Eliot in seeking to reinstate the certainties that had been lost, either through a religious revival or a return to classicism, but neither was there a nihilistic sense that existence is forever shattered and we have to put up with it in some kind of *danse macabre* over the corpse of humanist certainty. Instead, out of the dialectical processes he found in diverse sources Read sought to formulate a new kind of existence.

I do, of course, recognise that in this short book I have had to conflate, to some extent, the terms romanticism and idealism in a way that might offend philologists. If this is seen as an injudicious compromise from a philosophical point of view, there are good reasons for doing so from an historical vantage point. As a first defence I would echo Nicholas Boyle's comment that it is impossible for anyone to sufficiently differentiate romanticism from idealism while there is no generally accepted definition of romanticism.[26] And although there are arguments to be made for a difference between idealism and romanticism, there is also a family resemblance.[27] This stems partly from a shared relationship to the writings of Kant,[28] but there is also a shared roster of personnel in the ranks of the early nineteenth-century romantic and idealist philosophers in Germany, including Novalis, Fichte, Schlegel, Schleiermacher and Schelling, any one of whom is at times labelled a romanticist, or an idealist, or both. As this implies, there is a close proximity between romanticist and idealist ideas. Indeed, one commentator has described the differences between romantic philosophy and idealism as so slight it resembles what Sigmund

---

26 Nicholas Boyle, 'General Instroduction: the Eighteenth and Nineteenth Centuries' in Karl Ameriks (ed), *The Impact of Idealism: Volume 1, Philosophy and Natural Sciences: The Legacy of Post-Kantian German Thought* (Cambridge: Cambridge University Press, 2013) unpaginated

27 See Andrew Bowie, 'German Idealism and the Arts', in Karl Ameriks (ed.), *The Cambridge Companion to German Idealism* (Cambridge: Cambridge University Press, 2000) 250 and *passim*

28 See Sebastian Gardner, 'From Kant to Post-Kantian Idealism', in *Aristotelian Society Supplementary Volume,* vol. 76, no 1, July 2002, 211-28

Freud called, 'the narcissism of minor differences.'[29] However, more significant in relation to Read is the undeniable influence of idealist philosophers on romantic art and literature, particularly in Britain,[30] a point noted by Read himself.[31] From this influence we might consider British, and probably German, romanticism in both the visual and literary arts to be the artistic manifestation of idealism in philosophy. Certainly that is how Read appears to have seen this issue and it is a policy I have chosen to continue at the risk of fuelling the perennial dislike philosophers seem to have for art historians playing fast and loose with philosophical ideas.

Acknowledgements and thanks are due to a number of people and organisations. First and foremost to Professor Fintan Cullen, and also to Margaret Boyd and Liz Jennings, all at at the

29 John H. Smith, 'Living Religion as Vanishing Mediator: Schleiermacher, Early Romanticism, and Idealism', in *The German Quarterly*, vol. 84, no. 2, Spring 2011,148

30 An extensive discussion of this is available from Mark Kippermann in *Beyond Enchantment: German Idealism and English Romantic Poetry* (Philadelphia: University of Pennsylvania Press, 1986)

31 Herbert Read, *The True Voice of Feeling* (London: Faber, 1953) 165f

University of Nottingham. Also my thanks go to Emma Hardy, and Stass Paraskos, Mary Paraskos and Christopher Paraskos, and to Tom Steele, and Norbert Lynton.

I would like to pay especial thanks to Herbert Read's family for their assistance, in particular Benedict Read. Institutional thanks go to the libraries and their staffs at the British Library, London; the University of Leeds Brotherton Library, and in particular Special Collections; the University of Nottingham Library; the National Art Library at the Victoria and Albert Museum; the Special Collections Library at the University of British Columbia: and the Westminster Art Library in London.

Herbert Read:
Art and Idealism

EPISTEMIC TRAUMA

One of the ways to characterise the modernist period is as a time when the old certainties embodied in an historic humanist model of reality were swept away in the face of social, cultural and intellectual developments. These ranged from the rise of urban living and loss of religious faith, to the formulation of theories of evolution and relativity and the anti-bourgeois philosophy of Friedrich Nietzsche. Responses to this were diverse, and included not only various collective and social factors, but the many individual experiences of people at the time. To encompass both the collective and the individual experience of the shattering or fragmentation of what had seemed immutable beliefs, the term 'epistemic trauma' has been suggested.[32] It is a term we will use here to describe the consequences of this revolutionary experience.

The notion of an epistemic trauma affecting not only society but individuals is certainly useful in relation to Herbert Read, not least because of its almost psychoanalytical connotations. In Read there was early on an interest in the work of psychotherapists like Sigmund Freud and Carl Gustav Jung, whose mission in their psychotherapies was very much to alleviate this epistemic trauma, which manifested itself as the neurosis or psychosis afflicting their patients. But for Read the social aspect of epistemic trauma was also important, a fact that attracted him not only to the work of Freud and Jung, but to the philosophies of idealism and existentialism, and the politics of anarchism.

As we shall see, Read's tendency was always to synthesise ideas from diverse sources, hybridising them into new forms,

---

32 Thomas Vargish and Delo Mook, *Inside Cubism* (New Haven and London: Yale University Press, 1999) 35

some of which the authors of his original material would undoubtedly have rejected. Later on we will see this in action when Read tried in the 1930s to reconcile the mutually hostile camps of the Constructivists and Surrealists in the art world. Read called the process of synthesis 'reintegration', a term he borrowed from Jung.

The need for reintegration arose from the collapse of faith in the certainties of life which had made people feel, in relative terms at least, at ease in the world. As Read stated, these stemmed from:

> the death of God (to use Nietzsche's phrase to summarise a depersonalisation of religion, not least striking in those who still believe in God); the surrender of individual conscience to the tyranny of the State; the consequent growth of mass violence and mass destruction; the abdication of philosophy, its

retreat into verbal analysis; the inadequacy of scientific rationalism; and finally the dehumanisation of art.[33]

A more standard model of the shattering of humanist certainty would include the writings not only of Nietzsche, but the work of Charles Darwin, Freud and Albert Einstein as factors, along with rapid urbanisation and industrialisation, and a succession of traumatic European wars, starting with the Crimean War in the 1850s, the Franco-Prussian War in the 1870s and ultimately the First World War of 1914 to 1918. Out of this maelstrom the previously coherent sense of human selfhood was shattered, which Read characterised specifically as a breakdown in the relationship between our sense of inner self and the world around us. This immediately gave Read two points of opposition, each standing in contradiction to the other; the self on one side and the external world on the other. Crucially it also gave Read

33 Herbert Read, *The Forms of Things Unknown* (London: Faber, 1960) 153

a mission, namely the need to reintegrate these oppositional forces in order to facilitate human happiness.

This is an extraordinary statement to make about any art or literary critic. It is almost inconceivable that one could talk about a desire to bring about human happiness lying at the heart of the work of, say, Kenneth Clarke, Clement Greenberg or Terry Eagleton. But it is there in the art and literary criticism of Herbert Read, and for Read the desire to ameliorate the epistemic trauma of modernity required a new theory of synthesis.

At the start of the twentieth century, psychotherapy seemed to offer one theory and even a method for reintegration, at least on an individual level. But as has been suggested, Read's ambition was not simply for individual reintegration. It was for a complete reintegration of society. For this the straightforward use of Freudianism, or other forms of psychotherapy, would be insufficient. A more ambitious theory was needed which would encompass not only aspects of psychotherapy, but art, politics and, of course, philosophy.

READ AND IDEALISM

Read developed an early interest in German idealist philosophy. His first encounter with it was almost certainly at the Leeds Arts Club, a radical modernist group he joined around 1911 or 1912, where the members debated the latest artistic, political and social theories coming out of Europe, and even enjoyed displays of abstract expressionist paintings by artists such as Wassily Kandinsky. Here too the writings of Nietzsche were extremely influential.[34] Admittedly Nietzsche was not a straightforward idealist and so it is not surprising to find periods in his life when Read was explicitly hostile to idealism whilst remaining an admirer of Nietzsche. We will explore this

---

34 Tom Steele, *Alfred Orage and the Leeds Arts Club 1893-1923* (Mitcham: Orage Press, 2009) 218f

in more detail later on, but at this point it is worth spending some time looking at how Read began to develop a theory of culture that was re-integrationist or synthesist and its relationship to philosophical idealism.

Although Read was born at the very end of the nineteenth century, the origin of his interest in idealist philosophy lay in the debates that raged during the nineteenth century between advocates of classicism and romanticism. By revisiting these earlier debates Read developed a critical framework that he was able to apply to the modernist art and culture of the twentieth century. But in using the nineteenth-century debate as his starting point Read also inherited some of the inherent problems of that debate. Most notable was the question what one meant by the terms 'classicism', 'idealism' and 'romanticism'. As Read himself noted, the supposed classicism of the German writer Goethe was often more romantic than romanticism,[35] and this nomial slippage was not unusual with

---

35 Herbert Read, *Annals of Innocence and Experience* (London: Faber and Faber, 1940) 132-5.

the terms.[36] In a wonderfully succinct description, written in 1962, on the problem of defining romanticism Herbert Schueller stated:

> What explanations have we not heard? Romanticism is the resurgence of medievalism, we are told, or the medievalizing tendency; in contrast to health and classicism, it is sickness; it is emotion in full display, though primarily emotion not about form, but about a content; it can reveal the infinite, in the direction of which it tends; it is the reconciliation of opposites and the manifestation of free will as compared with necessity; it is the rediscovery of nature, and at the same time a kind of religious pantheism; it is the renascence of wonder, and while it involves freedom, it also results in gloom and disaffection. It stresses subjectivity, but at the same time is allied with the

---

36 It was noted in relation to romanticism in 1925 by Paul Kaufman in an essay entitled 'Defining Romanticism: A Survey and a Program', published in *Modern Language Notes,* vol. 40, no. 4, April, 1925, 193-204

spurious objectivity of science. Escaping into what the individual desires, it celebrates suicide, which is the apparent denial of life, though it also celebrates life in its richness and multiplicity. A kind of neoplatonism, a mysticism, a transcendentalism, it yet attempts to grapple with the phenomenon of perception and to discover the truths hiding behind it.[37]

To anyone accustomed to Read's work some of Schueller's definitions of romanticism will be familiar, and we will return to them again.

In Read's earliest understanding of the term, romanticism was certainly held as being in contrast to classicism, and it was also associated with the emotional, or rather the inner psychological, faculties of humankind. Although Read inherited these ideas from nineteenth century writers on romanticism, with his integrationist tendencies he was not satisfied with

37 Herbert M. Schueller, 'Romanticism Reconsidered', in *The Journal of Aesthetics and Art Criticism,* vol. 20, no. 4, Summer, 1962, 359-60

leaving romanticism and classicism as distinct and opposing categories, and in attempting to synthesise them into a new entity Read appears to have drawn on the work of Charles Herford. Although little known today, at the end of the nineteenth and into the twentieth century Herford was a well known professor of English, first at the University College of Wales, Aberystwyth, and then at the Victoria University of Manchester. In his writings he straddled the crossover from the relative simplicity of the nineteenth-century conception of romanticism and classicism being opposites, to more complex ideas prefiguring those of Read.

Initially Herford claimed romanticism was associated with, 'that sort of charm... which suggests unreality'. It signified emotional, unconscious and subjective faculties and, 'an attraction to the sensuous, vivid, fantastic, even unreal, [in] art'. In contrasting this with classicism he suggested, 'Unity, subordination, harmony, are among the most obvious attributes of classicism: diversity, picturesqueness and a sort of emulous self-assertion of each part, are conventionally assigned to the romantic.'[38] In this definition Herford saw classicism and romanticism as mutually exclusive theories operating in a binary system of 'unity, subordination [and] harmony' versus the 'sensuous, vivid [and] fantastic'. If classicism was a conception of reality being 'out there', romanticism was the 'unreal' imagination inside the mind.

In 1922 Herford modified this distinction, providing a rather different definition of romanticism which appears in Schueller's list under the guise of 'the reconciliation of opposites'. In doing so Herford moves us closer to Read. Herford wrote: 'In the historic romanticism of the eighteenth and nineteenth centuries, at least, inner vision and outer perception did not operate in detached compartments.'[39] In stating this Herford was modifying his earlier definitions quite

---

38 C.H. Herford, *The Essential Characteristics of the Romantic and Classical Styles* (Cambridge: Cambridge University Press, 1880) 1-8.

39 C.H. Herford 'Romanticism in the Modern World', in G.C. Moore Smith (ed.), *Essays and Studies by Members of the English Association,* vol. III (Oxford: Oxford University Press, 1922) 122.

dramatically, so that romanticism was no longer a straightforward antithesis to classicism, but a hybrid category in which the 'classical' reality of the external world and the hitherto 'romantic' unreality of the internal world were in some way unified. It was this synthesised definition of romanticism that Read picked up,[40] and rather than jettison the problematic term romanticism completely he also followed Herford's methodology in attempting to redefine romanticism to fit in with his new integrationist schema. This left Read, as it did Herford, with the difficulty in explaining that a newly defined romanticism was in fact the unifier of both classicism and the old way of defining romanticism. In more straightforward terms the newly defined romanticism was a theory that aimed to reintegrate or synthesise classical 'outscape' and romantic 'inscape' into a new coherent whole.[41]

---

40 Read is known to have owned Herford's book *The Age of Wordsworth* (London: Bell and Sons, 1924).

41 They were not alone in doing this at this time, as the example of Lascelles Abercrombie shows. Abercrombie too saw romanticism as a philosophy that bridged the self and the non-self. See Lascelles Abercrombie, *Romanticism* (London: Martin Secker, 1926) 80.

Emerging from this was a belief in Read that neither a classical nor a romantic approach to life, society or indeed art was sufficient on its own. As separate entities they each served to atomise the human experience. Classicism alone might lead to knowledge, Read reasoned, but the idea such knowledge would be absolute was attacked by him as a 'radical empiricism' that had become increasingly paramount in both science and philosophy since the eighteenth century.[42] Similarly the old definition of romanticism alone was insufficient in Read's schema as it was too personal and individual to have social relevance.[43]

As we have heard, Read's desire to integrate classicism and romanticism was not simply a philosophical issue. As part of his synthesising tendency Read drew on the work of Freud and Jung, suggesting it was almost a health issue. Freud's notion that psychiatric illness was a manifestation of the body's inability to

42 See Herbert Read, *Forms of Things Unknown* (London: Faber and Faber, 1960) 6f.

43 See Read's comments on Coleridge's poem 'Dejection', in Herbert Read, *The True Voice of Feeling* (London: Faber and Faber, 1953) 33-36.

reconcile two contradictory impulses or desires can be correlated neatly to the need to reconcile classicism and romanticism. But Read also mapped Jung's dichotomy of the introvert and extrovert personality onto his system, equating the introvert with romanticism and the extrovert with classicism. In doing so Read quoted André Gide: 'It is important to remember that the struggle between classicism and romanticism also exists inside each mind.'[44]

THE WAVERING '20s

Although we might imagine Read in the 1920s was a firm advocate of something we might call idealist, or at the very least romantic, philosophy the truth is he was still developing his ideas, and in doing so wavered, sometimes wildly, in his beliefs. This is shown by Read's encounters at the time with the work

44 *Ibid*, 221

of the English classicist philosopher T.E. Hulme, and the German idealist philosopher Wilhelm Worringer.

Hulme had died in 1917 on the battlefields of the First World War and in 1921 Read was asked by the editor of the *New Age* newspaper, Alfred Orage, to edit Hulme's papers for publication.[45] As we have seen, the classicism-romanticism debate was commonplace enough for Read to have a working knowledge of it. But Hulme presented Read with a problem as he had been a vehement classicist philosopher who showed a clear admiration for an idealist one.

Hulme was adamant that classicism and romanticism were distinct ways of conceptualising consciousness and reality and that the two were mutually exclusive. In Hulme's own metaphor the romantic saw human nature as akin to a well from which water could be drawn eternally, whilst for the classicist it was more like the finite volume of a bucket. Hulme wrote: 'Here is the root of all romanticism: that man, the

45 These were published in 1924 under the title *Speculations*. See James King, *The Last Modern* (London: Weidenfeld and Nicolson, 1990) 72-3

individual, is an infinite reservoir of possibility; and if you can so rearrange society by the destruction of oppressive order then these possibilities will have a chance and you will get Progress.' This was in fact a good definition of the romantic anarchism Read would later endorse. In classicism on the other hand: 'Man is an extraordinarily fixed and limited animal whose nature is absolutely constant. It is only by tradition and organisation that anything decent can be got out of him.'[46] In more bombastic mode Hulme predicted that: 'After a hundred years of romanticism we are in for a classical revival'. Although this would not necessarily see 'a return to Pope', and might not even be recognised as a classical style, it would possess the essential characteristics of classicism.[47]

Clearly Hulme's classicism would be difficult for Read to reconcile with his still developing interest in anarchism, but despite Hulme's position appearing to be straightforwardly

46 T.E. Hulme, *Speculations,* edited by Herbert Read (London: Routledge, 1924) 116

47 *Ibid,* 113

classicist his claim the new classicism 'might not even be recognised as a classical style' suggests a more complex situation. Hulme was certainly a complex and often wilfully contradictory character[48] who, along with Ezra Pound and Percy Wyndham Lewis, helped to define the extreme edge of pre-First World War modernism in Britain. This is borne out by Hulme's admiration for the work of the French philosopher Henri Bergson. As Karl Ameriks suggests, Bergson was in many ways an idealist philosopher,[49] although he too has been seen as a classicist, depending on the take of his work by different readers.[50] Either way, Bergson was not the zealous pro-classicist we might expect Hulme to admire. Worringer too is arguably more a romanticist, or at least idealist, thinker than Hulme ever sought to be. According to Worringer, although animals might

48 See Mary Ann Gillies, *Henri Bergson and British Modernism* (Montreal, McGill-Queen's University Press, 1996) 43f and *passim*

49 See Karl Ameriks's introduction to Karl Ameriks (ed), *The Impact of Idealism: Volume 1, Philosophy and Natural Sciences: The Legacy of Post-Kantian German Thought* (Cambridge: Cambridge University Press, 2013) unpaginated

50 For a summary of this see Matthew Gibson, 'Contradictory Images: The Conflicting Influences of Henry Bergson and William James on T. E. Hulme, and the Consequences for Imagism, *Review of English Studies,* vol. 62, 2011, 275-77

exist in the fluvial world of actuality, humankind was forced as a payoff for consciousness to fabricate a more fixed reality to stand in for the actuality that the senses experienced. The mind did this in order to achieve psychological ease. In *Form in Gothic*, translated into English by Read in 1927, Worringer presented the world outside the human mind as terrible and terrifying, an arbitrary and shifting force that is for the most part hostile. The transcendence of this actuality to achieve a fabricated mental image of reality placed Worringer firmly in the idealist camp. Humankind was, and is, forced for its own mental wellbeing to convert, 'what was living and arbitrary in [its] ceaselessly fluctuating visual impressions into invariable symbols of an intuitive and abstract kind'.[51]

This theme also appeared in Worringer's book *Abstraction and Empathy*. 'The original artistic impulse has nothing to do with the imitation of nature,' Worringer stated. 'This impulse is in search of pure abstraction as the sole possibility of finding

51 Wilhelm Worringer, *Form in Gothic* (London: Putnams, 1927) 29

rest amidst the confusion and obscurity of the image of the world, and it creates a purely geometric abstraction starting with itself, in a purely instinctive manner.'[52] Again in idealist mode Worringer suggested that when the mind attempted to establish reality it always started with itself, 'in a purely instinctive manner'. This meant reality was not something fixed and simply waiting to be experienced as the truth, it was a construction by and within the mind.

Hulme's admiration for Worringer was clearly a problem for Read in editing *Speculations* as it suggested a fundamental contradiction lay at the heart of Hulme's thinking. To try to counter this charge Read later suggested Hulme's ideas were in a state of flux at the time, 'as his collected papers…sufficiently prove.'[53] For Read Hulme's categoric dismissal of romanticism in favour of classicism was too difficult to reconcile with Worringer's notion that the romantic and classical were both

52 Wilhelm Worringer, *Abstraction and Empathy,* first published in German in 1908, quoted in Ferrier *et al., Art of Our Century: The Chronicle of Western Art 1900 to the Present* (New York: Prentice Hall, 1988) 94

53 Herbert Read, *Annals of Innocence and Experience* (London: Faber and Faber, 1940) 135

part of the human psyche and this may explain why Read chose to ignore Worringer completely in his introduction to *Speculations*.[54]

Although Read claimed Hulme's ideas had been in a state of flux, so were his own during the 1920s, and the apparent declaration of a romantic affiliation, in essays such as 'Psycho-Analysis and the Critic', written in 1925, was contemporary with frequent statements opposed to romanticism. For example, only a year before writing 'Psycho-Analysis and the Critic' Read claimed, in a review of Irving Babbitt's *Democracy and Leadership*, that Babbitt's motive was always: 'the re-establishment of humanistic standards in place of the utilitarian, humanitarian or romantic confusions so prevalent everywhere to-day.'[55] A few years later, in 1930, Read wrote: 'the classicist is also a realist, and the war has left behind a generation of realists who have not yet made themselves felt. When realism and classicism at

54 This was in contrast to the inclusion of other philosophers such as Friedrich Nietzsche, Henri Bergson and Georges Sorel.

55 Herbert Read, review of Irving Babbitt, *Democracy and Leadership,* in *The Criterion,* vol.3, no.9, 1924, 129

last join forces, the eclipse of romanticism and sentimentalism will be complete.'[56]

Andrew Causey has suggested that Read's pro-classical attitude during the 1920s was strongly influenced by his friendship with T.S. Eliot and association with the writers who congregated around the journal *The Criterion*. As Causey states, Eliot's preference was for: 'a stern culture, anti-popular and concerned – outwardly at least – more with standards than experiment. With watchwords like order, authority, tradition and the impersonal, it saw itself as reacting to the chaos in cultural and spiritual values that were perceived as resulting from the nineteenth-century's twin legacies of mass materialism and romantic individualism.'[57] Consequently Read might have had two reasons to ignore Worringer in his introduction to Hulme. One stemmed from a need to create a sense of

56 Herbert Read, *Julien Benda and the New Humanism* (Seattle, University of Washington, 1930) 15

57 See Andrew Causey 'Herbert Read and the North European Tradition', in Benedict Read and David Thistlewood, *Herbert Read: A British Vision of World Art* (London: Lund Humphries, 1993) 38ff

coherency in Hulme's writings, but the other came from his own flirtation with the classicism of Babbitt, Benda and Eliot.

Despite this, Read abandoned relatively quickly the more extremist forms of classicism of the 1920s and so it is questionable how heartfelt his adoption of classicism really was. Although he declared at one point to be a disciple of another classicist, Georges Sorel, Read later claimed: 'I only swallowed [Sorel's] doctrine of classicism because it seemed to me to be more romantic than romanticism itself – rather like Goethe's classicism'. Similarly in Sorel's exclusion of art from ideological control Read claimed there was: 'the whole of my subsequent elaboration of the doctrine of romantic art'.[58] These were not simply disingenuous justifications after the event, as Read was happy to admit that he had adopted a classicist approach in the 1920s. But as his knowledge of art and theory grew he came to believe classicism was not the antonym to romanticism. Instead

58 Herbert Read, *Annals of Innocence and Experience* (London: Faber and Faber, 1940) 132-5

both were embodied within romanticism, much as Herford had suggested.

If the 1920s can be characterised as a confused time for Read's advocacy of an idealist aesthetic, the change from the 1920s to the 1930s was dramatic. This saw Read shift into a mode of thought that was to remain more or less consistent for the rest of his life. It was dramatic enough to elicit comment at the time from C. Price Jones in a review of Read's book *Art and Society*. According to Price Jones Read had made: 'a shift of intellectual attitude from a rationalist position to one more sympathetic to the claims of intuition and instinct'.[59]

One can see Read struggling with the implications of this shift in his 1933 book *Art Now* in which there were still several anti-idealist declarations, similar to those made in the 1920s, but also a number of anti-classicist statements. In anti-idealist mode Read stated: 'I have never been able to believe that the idealistic conception of art, developed on a basis of Kant's aesthetic by

59 Jones, G. Price, review of Herbert Read, *Art and Society*, in *The Burlington Magazine*, vol. 71, no. 412, July 1931, 57-8.

writers like Schiller, Fichte and Schelling, and given a more popular romantic expression by poets such as Richter and Novalis, is worth the time that would be involved in mastering its mysteries.'[60] At the same time Read held an anti-classicist view that western art had from the Renaissance until the end of the nineteenth century ceased to be creative as it had became over-intellectualised. While art could flourish, 'in a rank and barbaric manner from an excess of animal vitality', it withered and died, 'in the arid excess of reason'.[61] This attack on the intellectualisation of art is even more remarkable given Read's praise of Julien Benda for his 'classicism, order and intelligence' only three years earlier.[62]

Further evidence that Read was shifting his philosophical position is provided by his increasing use of the ideas of Samuel Taylor Coleridge. Although more well-known as a poet,

60 Herbert Read, *Art Now* (London: Faber and Faber, 1933) 35

61 Herbert Read, *Art Now* (London: Faber and Faber, 1933) 28-32. Read's statement here that classicism made of art 'an abstract idea' was an instance of him attacking classicism by quoting Reynold's own words in support of classicism.

62 Read, *Julien Benda and the New Humanism* (Seattle: University of Washington, 1930) 10ff

Coleridge was a notable philosopher who effectively introduced the ideas of the German idealist philosopher Friedrich von Schelling into England. Read made extensive use of Coleridge as early as 1928 in *English Prose Style*,[63] and after 1930 cited him frequently.[64] By turning to Coleridge Read was intimating a much firmer affiliation with a form of romantic dialectical reasoning. In *English Prose Style*, for example, he noted that 'dialectical tension' was a well-known literary convention evident in the practice of thesis and antithesis. Read wrote: 'Antithesis operates by a tension or suspense between two ideas; the sentence becomes a balance between equal but opposite forces'.[65] Read also used Coleridge to distance himself from Hulme's earlier conception of the classicism-romanticism debate by adopting Coleridge's suggestion that there was

63 Herbert Read, *English Prose Style* (London: Bell, 1928) 42 and *passim*.

64 For example, see Read's use of Coleridge in *Wordsworth* (London: Jonathan Cape, 1930) 17 and *passim*; in *True Voice* 15f; in *Essays in Literary Criticism* (London: Faber, 1951; 1969 reprint) 126 and *passim*, and in *Icon and Idea* (London: Faber, 1955) 39 and *passim*. The version in *The True Voice of Feeling* had previously been published as the 'Coleridge as Critic', in *Sewanee Review*, vol. LVI (1948) 597-624, and this was republished by Faber in 1949 as a pamphlet, before becoming a chapter in *The True Voice of Feeling* in 1953.

65 Herbert Read, *English Prose Style* (London: Bell, 1928), 42

classicism and romanticism in all works of art, and that it was the relative predominance of classical 'order or judgement' compared to romantic 'emotion or feeling' that determined whether that work was prosaic or poetic.[66]

The decisive shift in Read's intellectual parameters during the 1930s was followed by a stabilisation of his views. The consistency of Read from the mid-1930s onwards is in fact remarkable, so that his adoption of Coleridge's version of the classicism-romanticism debate in *English Prose Style* could be relocated to almost any point in his later life. This is shown by *The True Voice of Feeling*, written over twenty years after *English Prose Style*, where Read discussed Coleridge in ways remarkably similar to his approach in *English Prose Style*.[67] Although his later usage might have been more sophisticated, and have more authorities to back it up, the basic premise remained the same. Read's discussion of thesis and antithesis also re-emerged in

66 *Ibid,* 136-44

67 Herbert Read, *The True Voice of Feeling* (London: Faber and Faber, 1953) 174

1952 in *The Philosophy of Modern Art,* again using the same language as well as the same concepts that appeared in *English Prose Style.*[68]

Such consistency can also be seen in the way Read's philosophy spilled over into other areas of his life, becoming part of a total system rather than a discrete way of conceptualising art and literature. In his unwillingness to accept the classicist idea of a fixed external reality that is received passively by the human mind it was logical for Read to reject also the idea that people should be passive receptacles of external political ideologies. This philosophical grounding meant Read's dislike of capitalism was not only due to the inequities that capitalism created, but to the way in which capitalism imposed on people a particular, bourgeois, view of reality. Although Marxism also proposed stripping away bourgeois reality to reveal the true reality, Read joined anarchists in criticising Marxism too for what Marxist writers such as Georg

68 Herbert Read, *The Philosophy of Modern Art* (London: Faber, 1952) 107-9

Lukács believed was the nature of that true reality.[69] Rather than freeing the individual from any external imposition of reality, in Read's eyes Marxism simply sought to strip away one of the ideologies that had historically masked the economic reality of existence and replace it with a new ideology of its own. The denial, implicit in Read's romantic idealism, of the possibility of experiencing true reality directly was clearly incompatible with Marxism as idealist reality was necessarily created through an organic and unpredictable dialectical process that denied the possibility of any fixed reality. Anything that claimed to be a fixed and irreplaceable truth, including Marxism, was thus no more than the replacement of one externally-imposed ideology with another. This was to become the principle on which Read opposed all the dominant political movements of the twentieth century, including Marxism, fascism and bourgeois liberalism, as he came to see the problem of

---

69 See Georg Lukàcs, 'Reification and the Consciousness of the Proletariat' in Georg Lukàcs, *History and Class Consciousness: Studies in Marxist Dialectics,* trans. Rodney Livingstone (London: Merlin, 1971) 83

society from an anarchist perspective. The problem was not which ideology humankind lived under, but ideology itself.[70]

As we can see, Read's romantic idealism fitted well with his developing interest in anarchism. In both it was the embodied individual that gained a significant role in constructing reality. In a crude sense, Read's romantic idealism saw the individual defining his or her own reality much as anarchism saw each individual defining his or her own society.

As well as a developing interest in anarchism, it is notable that Read's shifts in philosophical and political affiliation during the early 1930s were simultaneous with his increasing interest in visual art. In the ten years between 1919 and 1929 Read averaged only one article on the visual arts a year, while in 1930 alone he averaged more than one a week. Although this did not represent a complete move away from literary criticism, it was an inversion of Read's ratio of literary to art criticism. Increasingly Read became known to the public as an art critic,

70 See Herbert Read, *To Hell with Culture and Other Essays* (London: Routledge, 1963) 38-48

and a spur to this was the commission in 1929 for Read to write a series of articles on art for the BBC's new weekly magazine *The Listener*. These articles were to become the core of one of Read's most perennial texts, *The Meaning of Art*.[71] More surprising was the role Eliot played in pushing Read towards art criticism. Eliot was, Read suggested, lost when it came to discussing the visual arts.[72] Although Read was comfortable discussing literature, he did acknowledge that he felt lost at times under Eliot's shadow, and he even went on to explore this theme in poetry. In the poem 'Lu Yün's Lament' Read imagined Lu Yün, the younger brother of the celebrated Chinese poet Lu Chi, bemoaning his fate at being born, 'in the shadow of a mighty oak'.[73] Yet it was Eliot who helped reorientate Read towards the visual arts by recommending him to Herbert Grierson for the Watson Gordon professorship in

71 First published in 1931 and still in print.

72 James King, *Herbert Read: The Last Modern* (London: Weidenfeld and Nicolson, 1990) 80

73 Herbert Read, *Moon's Farm and Other Poems* (London: Faber, 1955) 27

Fine Art at the University of Edinburgh, a post Read held from 1931 to 1933.[74]

That Read's increasing pursuit of art criticism was contemporary with his adoption of an idealist philosophical position and growing interest in anarchist politics seems significant. There was no clear-cut distinction between these activities in Read's mind, any more than there was between romantic idealism and psychoanalysis. Each seemed to point towards a common solution to the epistemic trauma of modernity. If that epistemic trauma led to a sense that reality was alienating and fragmented, the re-integrationist tendency of romanticism, whether in an anarchist political or an artistic form, had the potential to provide a way to ameliorate the pain of the individual and society and establish a kind of new reality without recourse to earlier discredited forms of humanism, as proposed by Eliot, or the neo-humanism of Marxism and fascism.

74 Grierson was himself Regius Professor of Rhetoric and English Literature at Edinburgh between 1915 and 1935. See James King, *Herbert Read: The Last Modern* (London: Weidenfeld and Nicolson, 1990) 96f

A COMPACT WITH PICASSO

In his account of Picasso's 1912 painting *The Aficionado*, Read stated:

> although the composition is derived from reality, there is no immediate perceptual image to be represented — rather a group of visual elements associated with memory-image. These associated elements may indeed, as Picasso has always insisted, be derived from visual experience; but the important distinction is that the painting becomes a free association of images (a construct of the visual imagination) and not the representation of a subject controlled by the laws of perspective.[75]

75 Herbert Read, *A Concise History of Modern Painting* (London: Thames and Hudson), 95-6. Cited in Thomas Vargish and Delo Mook, *Inside Cubism* (New Haven and London: Yale University Press, 1999) 34-5

This description fits well with Vargish and Mook's suggestion there had been a kind of collective social compact on the laws of perspective since the fifteenth century and on this, in Elizabeth Ermarth's phrase, a consensus had been reached in our culture.[76] This consensus had become the visual tradition, not simply in art but in our construction of reality itself, informing not only other art forms, including non-visual art forms such as literature, but our navigation of the world itself.[77] As a consequence, if that consensus had the authenticity of tradition behind it then, 'what compact,' Vargish and Mook ask, 'do we have with Picasso?' And equally, what right has an upstart artist like Picasso to dictate a new compact to us?[78]

In his rejection of tradition Picasso undoubtedly showed a kind of arrogance, an almost vicious selfishness, that appears

76 Elizabeth Ermarth, *Realism and Consensus in the English Novel* (Princeton: Princeton University Press, 1983) ix-x

77 *Ibid.*

78 Thomas Vargish and Delo Mook, *Inside Cubism* (New Haven and London: Yale University Press, 1999) 35

at best anti-social.[79] He was indeed proposing a new, and potentially egomaniacal, compact to a post-humanist world. From a Readian perspective Picasso was indeed proposing a new post-humanist compact to a post-humanist, or post-classical, world. In *The Aficionado* he committed an act of violence against the historic compact of the classical humanist tradition, with space, time and memory dissected and then fragments rearranged in a non-perspectival way akin to the non-linear narrative structures of many modernist novels. But for Read, despite the undoubted egomania he recognised was part of modernism, this was not necessarily anti-social. It could be seen as the herald of a new social compact, admittedly one that might have only a short life, but which was responsive through its very evanescence to the here and now. This made the *The Aficionado* emblematic of Read's belief the disintegrated compact of humanism, was reintegrated into a kind of new compact by art. Although the distinct images in the painting might be, as

79 See John Carroll, *Humanism: The Wreck of Western Culture* (London: Fontana Press, 1993) 182f

Read stated, 'derived from reality', they were rearranged into, 'a construct of the visual imagination'. As in romantic idealism the painting was the product of a dialectical encounter between the artist's egocentric inscape and the environment's social outscape, the latter heavily informed by the traditional values on which it was built. But as in anarchism the artist had denied the right of tradition to impose ideological constraints, such as classical perspective, modelling and linear narrative, onto the pictorial outcome of this encounter. For a romantic idealist and anarchist like Read, by asking what right had Picasso to dictate reality to the viewer, one was also questioning the right of tradition to do the same.

For Read this rejection of the traditional compact was a necessary precondition for the creation of art. There can be no art, he suggested, 'if we willingly and consciously submit our instinct of origination to traditional bonds and moral codes.'[80] As a consequence, for Picasso in creating a work like *The*

80 Herbert Read, *To Hell with Culture* (London: Routledge, 1963: 2002 reprint) 167

Aficionado the duty of the artist in creating an act of art necessitates the rejection of the historic compact in order to propose a new compact in the form of a work of art. In this way art comes to function as a kind of provisional statement of truth, or provisional reintegration of the self and actuality, rather than a singular and eternally fixed classical or humanist assertion of truth. In Read's formulation of modernism it was this experimental action, providing many possible answers in the search for truth that was the function of art in society.

If art was to function in this way then it was necessary to have places where this could happen. In psychoanalytical terms society needed a psychiatrist's couch'

After the Second World War Read was successful in co-founding a number of 'art and society' schemes that provided such a couch, including the Institute of Contemporary Arts (ICA) in London[81] and the Gregory Fellowships at the

81 Founded in 1947.

University of Leeds.[82] But before the war Read's efforts had been largely in vain. As early as 1931 he had used his inaugural lecture as Watson Gordon Professor of Fine Art at the University of Edinburgh to reject the suggestion that the modern artist and poet should be distanced from society,[83] arguing that universities should reinvent themselves as places where art and society could come together. There is reason to suspect Read was thinking of the relationship between the Leeds Arts Club and the University of Leeds in the 1910s and 1920s when he claimed this.[84] But the ambivalence and sometimes open hostility to Read in Edinburgh was perhaps an

---

82 The Gregory Fellowships were launched in 1949. The inauguration speech by the fellowships' benefactor, Peter Gregory, specifically described the purpose of the Gregory Fellowships as being to integrate the arts with the more utilitarian aspects of university education, for the benefit of the university, the students and society. See Hilary Diaper 'The Gregory Fellowships', in Benedict Read and David Thistlewood, *Herbert Read: A British Vision of World Art* (London: Lund Humphries, 1992) 134

83 Read had originally agreed with Benda's view that the artist should be distanced from society – see Herbert Read, review of *La Trahison des Clercs,* translated into English by Richard Aldington under the title *The Great Betrayal,* in *The Criterion,* vol. 3, 1928., 270-76

84 See Nanette Aldred, 'A Sufficient Flow of Vital Ideas: Herbert Read and the Flow of Ideas from the Leeds Arts Club to the ICA', in Michael Paraskos (ed), *Re-Reading Read: New Views on Herbert Read* (London: Freedom Press, 2007) 76f

indication that this idea did not go down well in the city.[85] In Edinburgh too Read had been active in attempts to establish an art school modelled on the German Bauhaus,[86] and in 1939 he encouraged Peggy Guggenheim to establish a centre for contemporary arts in London which he hoped would be a place for experimental art-making rather than a traditional museum.[87] Neither of these schemes came to fruition.

However, Read's greatest difficulty before the Second World War was not the failure to establish institutions for reintegration but the hostility of many artists, including a number of his friends, to the idea. This stemmed from their continuing adherence to a model of mutually-opposed classical and romantic art. In the 1930s the movements seen as the heirs to classicism and romanticism were respectively Constructivism and Surrealism, but neither camp was willing to countenance a

85 James King, *Herbert Read: The Last Modern* (London: Weidenfeld and Nicolson, 1990) 98-102

86 See David Thistlewood, *Formlessness and Form* (London: Routledge, 1984) 16

87 *Ibid*; and James King, *Herbert Read: The Last Modern* (London: Weidenfeld and Nicolson, 1990) 187

philosophical compromise with the other. This left Read in the almost unique position of being seen as a champion of both 'classical' Constructivism and 'romantic' Surrealism, becoming embroiled in both camps more or less simultaneously. In 1936 he was able to write positively on Constructivism in the journal *Axis,*[88] and on Surrealism in *The Left Review.*[89] Similarly, despite befriending the leading Constructivist sculptor Naum Gabo,[90] Read was to assist Roland Penrose in 1936 in staging the International Surrealist Exhibition in London. Then in 1937 he was back with the Constructivists contributing the essay 'The Faculty of Abstraction' to the publication *Circle: International Survey of Constructive Art,* edited by Gabo, Ben Nicholson and Leslie Martin.[91]

---

88 Herbert Read, 'Abstract Art: A Note for the Uninitiated', in *Axis,* no.5, 1936, 3

89 Herbert Read, 'Surrealism: the Dialectic of Art', in *Left Review,* vol.2, no.10, July 1936, 508

90 James King, *Herbert Read: The Last Modern* (London: Weidenfeld and Nicolson, 1990), 156

91 Herbert Read 'The Faculty of Abstraction', in Naum Gabo, Leslie Martin and Ben Nicholson (eds.), *Circle: International Survey of Constructive Art* (London: Faber, 1937)

If avant-gardism meant moving forward from the positions of the past, Read was clearly ahead of the game, having abandoned the classical-romantic dichotomy of the nineteenth century and replacing it with a new classical-romantic dialectic. Read's problem was that the artists with whom he mixed did not seem to agree. Despite having established a rather nice theory Read might have heeded the warning from Sorel: 'art has never adapted itself to the demands of theorists; it always upsets their plans for social harmony'.[92] This was certainly proven in the politically-charged atmosphere of the 1930s where Read's suggestions for a synthesis of opposites was not the way to win friends: in advocating and supporting both Constructivism and Surrealism Read faced criticism from both sides. Constructivist opposition to the 1936 Surrealist exhibition meant Read was left 'slightly out of favour' with Barbara Hepworth and Nicholson.[93] At the same time he was

---

92 Quoted in Herbert Read, *Annals of Innocence and Experience* (London: Faber and Faber, 1940) 135

93 James King, *Herbert Read: The Last Modern* (London: Weidenfeld and Nicolson, 1990) 164

viewed as a 'heretic' by several leading Surrealists to the extent that in 1939 he was expelled from the Surrealist group.[94] According to Eileen Agar this left Read feeling as if 'guns were being fired at from him from every side'.[95]

There is no denying that a tension was created between the two extremes represented by the Circle group and the Surrealist group, and that I was in the position of a circus rider with his feet planted astride two horses. I tried to argue, and I still believe, that such dialectical oppositions are good for the progress of art, and that the greatest artists…are great precisely because they can resolve such oppositions.[96]

94 George Woodcock, *Herbert Read: The Stream and the Source* (London: Faber and Faber, 1972) 26

95 Quoted in James King, *Herbert Read: The Last Modern* (London: Weidenfeld and Nicolson, 1990) 165

96 Herbert Read, 'A Nest of Gentle Artists', *Apollo,* vol. LXXVI, no. 7, 1962, reproduced in Benedict Read and David Thistlewood, *Herbert Read: A British Vision of World Art* (London: Lund Humphries, 1992) 60

By attempting to straddle two horses Read exposed the most serious problem with his theory. A new hybridised reality was supposed to be born from the meeting of opposites. But amid the hostility between the Constructivists and Surrealists it was difficult to see where any meeting point could exist as each remained a separate and rather stroppy animal. It was clear from the reactions of each camp that the self-justification of both the Surrealists and the Constructivists did not require the existence or acceptance of the validity of any opposition. This was a problem that was to sit at the heart of Read's 1933 book *Art Now*.

ART NOW AND THEN

In the 1933 edition of *Art Now* the problem of Constructivist and Surrealist synthesis was very apparent. It boiled down to a simple issue. The Constructivists and Surrealists did not like each other, or at least each other's ideas. Consequently the easiest solution for Read was to bypass any overt attempt at reconciliation and instead fall back on the old Hulmean concept of classicism and romanticism being mutually-opposed tendencies. In the manner he had previously ignored Worringer in his introduction to Hulme's *Speculations,* it was simply easier for Read to discuss the two tendencies he saw in modernism as being exclusive, rather than try to explore ideas of a new unified theory of modernism that would have antagonised both groups and been quickly rejected by them.[97] Nowhere was the retention of a Hulmean segregated model more apparent than in Read's suggestion that modern artists veer either towards 'Abstract Form', with the word abstract being a contemporary epithet for Constructivism, or towards 'Subjective Form' which was manifested in such movements as expressionism and

---

97 The motivation to avoid making enemies in the avant-garde in such a way might also have come from Read's relatively recent conversion to modern art criticism. It is moot, however, whether he was just uncertain as to which was the best path to follow, or he felt too vulnerable to make enemies so early on in his new career-path.

Surrealism. This classification was recognisably derived from the earlier division of classicism and romanticism.

In *Art Now* Read discussed the first of these, abstract form, in relation to the paintings of Paul Cézanne. Given the strong figurative element in Cézanne's art any suggestion he was an abstract painter appears counterintuitive but makes sense when the term abstract is returned to its etymological root as meaning 'to move away from'.[98] Abstract form was thus the moving away, or in idealist terms the externalisation, of form from the subjective self so that the subjective self was removed from the equation. This meant Read did not see abstraction as simply non-figurative art. Indeed, one could have non-figurative art that was non-abstract. Rather abstraction was an objectification of forms from the individual perceiving them and as such it was a denial of the self as a mediating factor in an object's existence. At a basic level this denial of subjectivity might also have been seen in naturalistic art, such as

98 See Andrew Causey, 'Herbert Read and Contemporary Art', in David Goodway, *Herbert Read Reassessed* (Liverpool: Liverpool University Press, 1998) 127

Impressionism, in which the artist's eye was believed to mimic the objectivity of a camera.[99] Despite Cézanne having an affinity with Impressionism's mimetic approach[100] it was not this that made his paintings objectified or abstract. Indeed, Cézanne's images were subject to variations in form, colour and paint handling that were clearly non-mimetic. These formal elements of composition might have appeared to be subjective, but according to Read the real purpose of them was, 'to achieve a pure state of consciousness before the natural object'. From this the object itself, and its relationship to other elements of its setting, such as parallel lines, repeated forms and common colour relationships, was revealed. Like impressionism this was an attempt, *apropos philosophical classicism,* to show reality without the subjectivity of the self, but it also had a political dimension, echoing the Marxist and anarchist belief that nineteenth-century naturalism, including scientific naturalism,

99 See Peter Childs, *Modernism* (London, Routledge, 2000) 109

100 Herbert Read, *Art Now* (London: Faber and Faber, 1933) 108

was a specifically bourgeois conception of reality masquerading as objectivity. Cezanne's art was thus an attempt to get behind or beyond this false class consciousness. If nineteenth-century naturalism reflected bourgeois ideas of objectivity, Cézanne's abstracting process revealed a more fundamental, and perhaps even truer, objective state. Read wrote that Cézanne, 'found himself giving to reality – to real things like mountains, trees and people – a structural configuration which was not the surface appearance of these things but rather the supporting geometry, their spatial depth, their immaculate colours devoid of highlights or shadows.'[101] According to Read: 'Cézanne staked everything on the inherent form,' and that form lay hidden in the object itself.[102]

A logical step for Read at this point might have been to move on to an artist such as Mondrian as an extreme example of abstract form, and in later editions of *Art Now* Read did

101 Herbert Read, *Icon and Idea* (London: Faber and Faber, 1955) 130

102 Herbert Read, *Art Now* (London: Faber and Faber, 1933) 104-5

indeed use Mondrian in this way. In Mondrian, Read later argued, the objectification is such that the subjective appearance of everyday reality is also stripped away, leaving only the underlying structures of lines and colours. Mondrian's art was, Read wrote, 'a search for what he called "a clear vision of true reality", an impersonal art "unconditioned by subjective feeling and conception."'[103] What was essential to Mondrian's practice was: 'a belief in a "true" reality, which was not the illusion of a scientific perceptual reality such as the Renaissance painters sought, but a basic unity achieved by "the abolition of all particular form," of all "particularities of form and natural colour," which merely "evoke subjective states of feeling."' In this Mondrian's language was, Read claimed, little different to that of Cézanne.[104]

The lack of any mention of Mondrian in the earlier 1933 edition of *Art Now* suggests Read was unfamiliar with Mondrian's

103 Herbert Read, *The Philosophy of Herbert Read, Modern Art* (London: Faber and Faber, 1952) 223-4

104 Herbert Read, *Icon and Idea* (London: Faber and Faber, 1955) 131

work at that time. This meant the section on abstract art was illustrated by works that only partly made Read's point and a lay audience might well have struggled (as they might now) to see the visual difference between the subjective forms of several of Read's Surrealist artists and the supposedly abstract objectification of Jean Metzinger's *City* or Fernand Léger's *Pear Tree Root,* both illustrated in the 1933 book. The exception to this was Sophie Taeuber-Arp's *Six Rooms* of 1932, in which the reduction of form to essential components of colour and geometric shape appeared to be fully realised.

Alongside abstract form in the 1933 *Art Now* was a theory of subjective form which was exemplified for Read by Picasso. Picasso was illustrated with eight works, by far the highest number for any artist in the book. However, in the text Read focused on Picasso's 1926 painting *Abstraction,*[105] a painting of a profile face, with elements that could be said to comprise an eye, eyebrows, nostrils and possibly a mouth to the left and

105 There are two works by Picasso with this title in the 1933 *Art Now,* but the one to which Read was referring was plate 106.

on the right-hand side forms which might be read figuratively as shadow, or as a second head. Despite these figurative elements Read claimed this painting showed, 'no parallel in visual experience'.[106] Instead its forms were sourced in the unconscious of the artist and appealed directly to the unconscious of the viewer.[107] As such it represented the opposite to abstract form, having no anchor in the objective actuality of the visible world.

At its most extreme, the theory of subjective form paralleled the claim by the idealist philosophers that the world is idea, an extreme denial of the existence of an objective, or at least knowable, external reality.[108] If external reality was a product of the internal mind, or a projection of the internal mind, it was reasonable to assume that the images of subjective form art were also products of the mind since there was no

106 Herbert Read, *Art Now* (London: Faber and Faber, 1933) 129

107 *Ibid,* 99-100

108 This is a paraphrase of Arthur Schopenhauer, see Schopenhauer, *Selected Essays* (London: Bell, 1914), 1-3. A copy of this was in Read's personal library, now in the Herbert Read Collection, University of Leeds Brotherton Library.

'out there' to reproduce. This would apply even if artworks appeared, as in the case of Picasso's *Abstraction,* to approximate human form. Subjective form was concerned with images drawn from the unconscious, or the inner world of the human mind and body.[109]

INTEGRAL VISION

If the 1933 *Art Now* appeared to justify an aspect of romantic idealism through Read's theory of subjective form, it is worth noting that the text was not fully resolved on the issue. Several idealist philosophers, including Schiller, Fichte, Schelling and Schopenhauer, came in for a drubbing in the book.[110] Yet as one would expect of a transitional text there were intimations of

109 This could be likened to the early Surrealist notion of disengagement of the mind exemplified by the experiments by artists such as Hans Arp, Joan Miro and Paul Klee in automatic drawing. See J. Gibson 'Surrealism Before Freud', in *Art Journal,* vol.46, no.1, 1987, 58

110 Herbert Read, *Art Now* (London: Faber and Faber, 1933) 35-9

change and suggestions that Read wanted to move toward a more synthetic dialectic, particularly in the use he made of the literary theorist Francesco de Sanctis.[111] De Sanctis had claimed:

> When a subject comes into the brain of a creative writer, it at once dissolves that part of reality which suggested it. The earthly images seem to fluctuate, like objects in a mass of vapour seen from above. The figures - the trees, the towers, the houses – disintegrate, becoming fragmentary. To create reality, a poet must first have the force to kill it.

Read effectively used de Sanctis to suggest that the mind created reality by bringing its internal resources together with the perception of external actuality. What we see is the integrationist strategy Read wanted to pursue in his art

111 Francesco de Sanctis's, *History of Italian Literature* (Oxford: Oxford University Press, 1930) was in Read's possession as a first edition, probably from 1930. Now in the Herbert Read Collection, University of Leeds Brotherton Library.

criticism making a tentative entrance via the back door of literary theory. Using de Sanctis Read was able to suggest the mind of the artist (or writer) necessarily engaged in an act of violence against the existing perception of reality, and in so doing fragmenting it. Those fragments became part the material from which to create a new reality, but the destructive process also opened up space in which to create that reality. In this way Read moved away from a theory that separated abstract form and subjective form to advocate a creative process that required the integration and interaction of both tendencies. The resulting image, Read suggested could be termed an 'integral vision'.[112]

If discussion of abstract and subjective form can be viewed as Read reporting the respective theories of Constructivism and Surrealism, the theory of integral vision was Read's independent theorisation of his desire for aesthetic unity. As we have seen, the theory had antecedents and parallels

112 Herbert Read, *Art Now* (London: Faber and Faber, 1933) 75

outside the art world, but Read was the first writer, at least since the Victorian art critic John Ruskin, to apply it in a systematic way to art. In the 1933 *Art Now* the theory might have been tentative, but the implication of artistic synthesis for the question of social reintegration was becoming apparent. In suggesting that the mind necessarily fragments experience in order to create new realities, de Sanctis provided Read not only with a guide to the unification of art, but a means to ameliorate the social disjuncture of modernity through an aesthetic process of reintegration.

While de Sanctis provided literary cover for Read to talk about the integration of classicism and romanticism, Read's use of Henri Matisse provided an example in visual art that was similarly sufficiently distanced from the London art world for him to get away with applying his radical integrationist ideas. By using Matisse Read took his theories outside the politically charged atmosphere of English modernism and freed them from sectarian attack. In *Art Now* Read reproduced three of Matisse's works, one of which, entitled *Girl in a Yellow Dress,* showed particularly well how he believed integral vision worked. Integral vision was a type of formalist theory in which the work of art was dependent not on narrative or symbolic elements, but on the harmony of the pictorial forms and their rendering. This was different to the formalism of Roger Fry and Clive Bell, or later that of Clement Greenberg, as it did not suggest formal properties were ends in themselves but a means to achieve a psychological, or perhaps even spiritual, state of harmony.

In pictorial terms Matisse's *Girl in a Yellow Dress* comprises a sketchily painted canvas in which a female figure is sat in front of a window. The glass panes of the window are open, but the shutters are closed, and the woman is sat upright, with her arms folded on her lap, wearing a yellow dress and green and orange hat. The image is overwhelmingly frontal, with the woman set face-on to the picture plane, and this frontal quality is emphasised both by her symmetry and by the closure of the shutters which prevents anything more than a very shallow illusion of depth. This forces everything shown in the picture towards the picture plane. The strong colours and sketchy finish add to this sense of shallow space, the first by their tendency to vie with each other for forward prominence and the second by the emphasis they place on the painted surface, thereby disrupting any illusion of naturalism. The colours, contortions of objects and manipulation of spatial illusion show Matisse denying comprehensively any adherence to the historic humanist model of reality. This might lead one to assume his image was not integrated at all, but a symptom of reality being fragmented. But when Matisse commented on his work he used phrases such as 'decorative', 'joyous' and 'harmonious'. In a well-known statement Matisse stated: 'What I dream of is an art of balance, of purity and serenity and devoid of depressing subject matter, an art which might be for every mental worker, be he a businessman or writer, like an appeasing influence, like a mental soother, something like a good armchair in which to rest from physical fatigue.'[113] Certainly this is not the language of a nihilist embracing chaos, but Read claimed Matisse's words had been misunderstood, as though he was trivialising his own art by calling it decorative and like an armchair.[114] Far from being trivial, Read saw in Matisse an indication that he was deeply concerned with a de Sanctis-like construction of a new and reintegrated sense of reality.[115] If the old classical-humanist reality had been rendered incoherent by modernity then that was simply the necessary violence involved in its destruction, like the violence of a broom as it sweeps up a chaotic mess. But an artist such as Matisse was attempting to move beyond the 'killing of reality' by reorganising the fragmented forms and experience into new compositions that were psychologically unified, and which could therefore be described as 'harmonious'. Harmonious was not used to denote prettiness, but something

113 Quoted in Herschel B. Chipp, *Theories of Modern Art* (Berkeley: University of California Press, 1968) 135

114 Herbert Read, *Art Now* (London: Faber and Faber, 1933) 73

115 *Ibid*, 77

more like reconstructed or resolved. As Read stated, this visual comfort could indeed be seen as, 'analogous to a good armchair in which one relaxes.'[116]

Looking at *Girl in a Yellow Dress* it is possible to say that Matisse achieves this by the very elements that seem to disrupt the humanist model of reality. The shallowness of the spatial plane places restrictions on where the viewer's gaze can go, so that the space out of the window and the middle-distance simply does not exist in terms of the picture's self-defined existence. This denial of any reference to space outside the painting forces the viewer to recognise the self-defined reality that is embodied in the painting so that it becomes a complete reality in itself. In the painting's reality nothing is hidden, and through the symmetrical form of the female figure, and overall compositional balance, nothing is discordant or unresolved.

At least that is one way of understanding the resolution Matisse came to. Discussing this matter with the British artist

116 *Ibid,* 79

Clive Head, on whom Matisse is a significant influence, Head suggested to me that there was also a kind of hidden order in Matisse which was manifest in the layering of multiple images. By this Head did not necessarily mean that Matisse superimposed images on top of each other, like a film negative repeatedly exposed to produce ghost images. Rather that his images often showed a multiplicity of views, suggesting movement through space and time, and also a playful instability, whereby one element in an image might stand for more than one thing.

A concept of playful instability has, as we shall see, specific resonance with the ideas of Read in relation to the deliberate incongruities set up by the Surrealists. But it is also easily identifiable in *Girl in a Yellow Dress* in elements such as the balcony. In the painting we can see in the shallow space through the window what appears to be the balustrade of a balcony, composed of orange stripes. Yet those orange stripes also continue inside the room, in the left arm of the woman, suggesting her arm is also the balcony, or no less bizarrely that her arm is somehow transparent allowing us to still see the orange stripes of the balcony behind it. I am tempted to suggest that this understanding of Matisse from Head fits in even more neatly than my own thoughts with what Read was beginning to understand about Matisse's work in *Art Now*. The self defined world that was created by Matisse was not a reassertion of classical order in the painting so as to provide a familiar 'comfortable armchair' for the viewer to relax into. This was not a return to humanist certainty as it had been posited by earlier generations at all. On the contrary it was a profoundly unfamiliar armchair, in which ambiguity (the arm that is also a balcony) could exist without invoking terror.[117]

Girl in a Yellow Dress remains a complete and self-contained reality, and because of that could be seen in Readian terms as a restorative to the epistemic trauma of modernity, but on those same terms its restorative power was not through a return to discredited humanist models of reality, it was

117 I am grateful to Clive Head for discussing this idea with me and sharing with me what I fully acknowledge is his understanding of Matisse. Conversation with Clive Head, 27 April 2013.

through its ability to construct a self-contained and integral new state of existence by being in itself a reconciling image. As Read noted, looking at a painting by Matisse our visual options are limited and, 'we must fix our gaze on a central point, hold that focus, and the rest of the picture, which to the analytical vision seems meaninglessly distorted, now falls into position, acquires its meaning and its due relationship.'[118] There can be little doubt this was a deliberate echo by Read of de Sanctis's claim that, 'the first real moment of creation in the tumultuous and fragmentary world is the moment when these fragments find a fixed point, a centre around which they can press.'[119]

118 Herbert Read, *Art Now* (London: Faber and Faber, 1933) 79

119 Francesco de Sanctis, quoted in Herbert Read, *Art Now* (London: Faber and Faber, 1933) 74-75

1936 AND ALL THAT

As we have seen the 1933 *Art Now* can be viewed as an
unresolved text due to Read's continuing equivocation over
idealist philosophers such of Schiller, Fichte and Schelling. This
can be viewed as the final gasp of Read's short-lived classicist
phase, prevalent in the 1920s. More significant is the unresolved
way in which Read dealt in the book with the discussion of
Constructivism and Surrealism. By avoiding the artists' own
labels, and renaming the Constructivists and Surrealists as
practitioners of abstract and subjective form, Read sought to
depoliticise their mutual hostility as much as philosophise their
aims. But this did not hide the fact he was attempting to
integrate them into a synthesist Readian theory that could
supersede their own perceptions of their art. Read was still
relatively new to art criticism in 1933 and this might have made
the thought of an open insistence on the primacy of his own
theory of art difficult. As a consequence the 1933 *Art Now*

appears to hold three competing theories – one classicist, one romanticist and one Readian, or rather synthesist, the last of these being somewhat oblique in its presentation.

When in 1936 Faber and Faber published a revised edition of *Art Now* much of the text remained intact, including Read's comments hostile to idealist philosophy.[120] Nonetheless the book was altered in significant ways. Changes to the labelling and organisation of the chapter headings were probably the most immediate indication that the 1936 *Art Now* was a different creature, but as a parallel reading of the two editions demonstrates there were other important changes. These were particularly apparent towards the end of the book, largely due to the final chapter dealing with the ever moving subject of contemporary art. But they reflected Read's increasing confidence with contemporary art between 1933 and 1936, a period that saw him move from the relative isolation of

120 Although this seems surprising, the phrases against Schelling *et al* remained intact for the entire life of the book, including the post-Second World War period when Read was lauding the same idealist philosophers in other books. Read's process of revision was not to rewrite a text completely, but incrementally with the result that later versions of a text did not necessary reflect Read's current opinions.

Edinburgh to the heart of British modernism in London's Hampstead.[121]

Nonetheless the pressure on Read to follow particular aesthetic lines was still immense. Much of this came from the artists themselves who continued to expect Read to promote them and their views and disavow their opponents.

This was not confined to the writing of *Art Now*. When in 1942 Read wrote an article for the periodical *Horizon*, in which he sought to declare the right of the critic to be free from partisanship, he came under fire from both Constructivists and the Surrealists, each opposed to Read giving space to the other. This prompted Read to write to the poet Henry Treece: 'My *Horizon* article has caused much perturbation among my "art" friends. It was meant as a declaration of independence, but from all sides they accuse me of desertion'.[122] On top of this Read

---

121 For Read's own account of this move see Read 'A Nest of Gentle Artists', in *Apollo,* reproduced in Benedict Read and David Thistlewood, *Herbert Read: A British Vision of World Art* (London: Lund Humphries, 1993) 60

122 Letter from Herbert Read to Henry Treece, 1942, quoted in James King, *Herbert Read: The Last Modern,* (London: Weidenfeld and Nicolson, 1990) 211-12

was subject to attempts at his re-education by artists. Much of this must have taken place unrecorded and behind closed doors in the studios of Hampstead, but a glimpse of what it was like for Read can be seen in a letter he received from Hepworth, again in 1942, in which Hepworth explained how Read misunderstood Constructivism in general and the work of the Constructivist sculptor Naum Gabo in particular.[123] Perhaps a similar re-education by Hepworth in person caused a subtle but significant change in the way Read described Kandinsky in *Art Now*. In 1933 Read stated that Kandinsky offered, 'one of the best *explanations* of abstract art'.[124] In 1936 this became, 'one of the best *approaches*' to it'.[125]

Despite circumstantial evidence that some artists succeeded in redirecting Read's writing, the changes to *Art Now* indicate a bid for independence based very much on Read's

123 Letter from Barbara Hepworth to Read, 1942, quoted in Thistlewood, *Herbert Read: Formlessness and Form* (London: Routledge, 1984) 86

124 Herbert Read, Art Now (London: Faber and Faber, 1933) 116

125 Herbert Read, Art Now (London: Faber and Faber, 1936) 116

developing interest in idealism and anarchism. The 1936 *Art Now* was an emphatic move away from a Hulmean conception of separate categories of classicism and romanticism towards a statement of synthesis. For Read this meant tackling the mutual hostility of Constructivism and Surrealism head on, which he did by suggesting that although both classicism and romanticism existed in their own right, each side should be willing to accept that, 'perfection may be achieved in the expression of either.'[126] More interesting is the way in which Read shifted the correlation of Constructivism and Surrealism with classicism and romanticism by suggesting that Surrealism was far closer to his developing redefinition of romantic idealism. Surrealism was not the art of the unconscious, Read suggested, but, 'the art of the complete mental personality: a synthesis of all its aspects and activities.'[127] This moved Surrealism from being a form of romanticism that was straightforwardly opposed to

---

126 Herbert Read, *Art Now* (London: Faber and Faber, 1936) 137

127 *Ibid.*

Constructivism, to a synthesising movement in its own right that possessed both classical and romantic qualities. Inevitably this left Constructivism somewhat out in the cold as being literally superseded by Surrealism, and so it is no wonder this period was peppered with attempts by Hepworth to re-educate Read. Notably these were directed towards persuading him that his synthesis of classicism and romanticism could be achieved through Constructivism instead of Surrealism. Hepworth argued that artists like Mondrian should not be even be labelled classical as it, 'entirely fails to describe the romance, daring and intensity of his work.'[128] That Hepworth wanted Read to consider Constructivism the true answer to his search for synthesis was also indicated by her 1934 statement in *Unit One* where she claimed to be inspired in her own work by contrasting industrial and natural forms: 'I see a blue aeroplane between a ploughed field and a green field, pylons in lovely

128 Letter from Barbara Hepworth to Herbert Read, December 1940, quoted in James King, *Herbert Read: The Last Modern,* (London: Weidenfeld and Nicolson, 1990) 187

juxtaposition with springy turf and trees of every stature. It is the relationship of these things that makes such loveliness.'[129]

Based on these examples Hepworth was right, her Constructivism did meet the requirements for synthesis. But in his own introduction for *Unit One* Read nailed his colours to a very different mast, the English Surrealism of Henry Moore. Consequently, in a new epilogue to the 1936 edition of *Art Now* Read not only set out the principles for a synthetic dialectic in an overt form, but established two artists as being the highest embodiment of it – Moore and Picasso – neither of whom came from the Constructivist camp. In doing so the Hulmean division between classicism and romanticism that had dominated the 1933 *Art Now* was finally swept away and replaced in the 1936 edition by the idea that there was a spectrum of artists, some of whom might be more romantic or classical than others, but all of whom operated within the same unified system.

---

129 Barbara Hepworth, artist's statement in Herbert Read (ed.), *Unit One* (London: Cassell, 1934) 20

In comparison to the 1933 edition this recategorisation of Picasso in the 1936 version was a significant shift. In 1933 Picasso was seen by Read as embodying the romanticist theory of subjective form, although even then Picasso was something of a Protean figure for Read.

> Picasso is an artist of many phases: he was one of the originators of the cubist school, and from time to time he makes excursions into the direct reproductive method of painting. But his most typical, and I think we can say his most consistent style is subjective. There are purer artists of this type... but Picasso, by virtue of his energy, his experimental verve, his réclame, must be considered first.[130]

In the 1936 version this evident refusal of Picasso to be categorised came to be seen by Read as fundamental to his art,

---

130 Herbert Read, *Art Now* (London: Faber and Faber, 1933) 121

not as evidence of romantic individualism, but of synthetic unification. In a new epilogue Read did reiterate the extremes of the dialectic, setting Mondrian against Dali, but he was also insistent that the space between them was, 'occupied by an unbroken series, in the centre of which we find artists like Picasso and Moore whom we cannot confidently assign to either school.' No longer was Read pulling his punches, insisting that such artists in the centre were, 'in possession of a fertile and powerful genius'.[131] For those artists, like Hepworth, whom Read declined to see occupying the centre ground this was an analysis that must have hurt.

ART AND ANGST

The recognition by Read that Picasso and Moore reconciled Hulme's seemingly incompatible extremes had far-reaching

---

131 Herbert Read, *Art Now* (London: Faber and Faber, 1936) 145-6

implications for his search for a means to correct the negative consequences of modernity. But it also linked Read to another great philosophical movement of his lifetime, post-war existentialism, a phenomenon with which he both identified and, rather like idealism, romanticism and classicism, sought to reformulate in his own way.

With hindsight, Read's connection to existentialism might have been predicted very early on in his career as a writer on art and culture. While it could have been augured through an analysis of Read's broader intellectual preferences during the 1930s and 1940s, it was presaged very directly in 1925 by his citation in 'Psycho-Analysis and the Critic'[132] of Andre Gide, a major influence on several existentialist philosophers.[133] When existentialism became widely recognised after the Second World War Read quickly concluded that his beliefs were

132 Herbert Read 'Psycho-analysis and the Critic', in *The Criterion,* vol.3, no.10, 1925, 221

133 Gide was a major influence on the post-Second World War existentialists, and in particular on Jean-Paul Sartre. See Jean-Paul Sartre 'Existentialism is a Humanism', a lecture delivered in Paris in 1946, reproduced in Walter Kaufman (ed.), *Existentialism from Dostoyevsky to Sartre* (New York: Meridian Publishing Company, 1979).

analogous to figures such as Sartre.[134] The speed with which Read did this was in fact remarkable. As early as 1948, in a lecture at the Johns Hopkins University in Baltimore, Read acknowledged affinities between himself and a number of idealist philosophers he now claimed to admire, such as Schelling and Coleridge, and existentialists such as Sartre. Read wrote:

> Schelling, no less than Coleridge, would have found [existentialism] very sympathetic, and perhaps it is to be expected that a modern existentialist should speak the same language as one of the earliest exponents of existentialist philosophy. I realise it may cause some surprise to hear Coleridge described as an existentialist, but I think it would not be difficult to justify the label. The origins of existentialism are usually traced to Kierkegaard;

134 Herbert Read, *Forms of Things Unknown* (London: Faber and Faber, 1960) 28

but a much better case can be made for Schelling, as Dr Bolman[135] has already pointed out.[136]

By this date the dismissal of idealism, found in both the 1933 and 1936 editions of *Art Now,* was gone from Read's writings, and in his 1948 lecture he sought to create a nexus of affiliations to which he belonged, incorporating not only idealism and existentialism, but anarchism. Indeed, he suggested, anarchism was a kind of existentialism.

If Coleridge and Schelling were unexpected existentialists, the link with anarchism will have surprised many British anarchists given the more standard association at the time of Sartre with the French Communist Party.[137] But according to

---

135 The Bolman reference is to Frederick de Wolfe Bolman's edition of Schelling's *The Ages of the World* (New York: Columbia University Press, 1942)

136 From Herbert Read, 'Coleridge as Critic', delivered as a lecture at Johns Hopkins University in 1948, reproduced in Herbert Read, *The True Voice of Feeling* (London: Faber and Faber, 1953) 180

137 Sartre declared himself no longer pro-Communist in November 1956 following the suppression of the Hungarian uprising by Soviet forces. See Donald D. Egbert, *Social Radicalism and the Arts* (New York: Alfred J. Knopf, 1970). Elias, Norbert, *The Court Society* (Oxford: Blackwell, 1969; reprinted 1983) 352

Read existentialists and anarchists shared a view of society which differentiated them from the Marxists:

> The difference is between those who believe that a particular ideal should predetermine man's existence (which is the official communist line) and those who believe (as existentialists and anarchists do) that the personality of man, that is to say his own subjectivity, is the existing reality and that the ideal is an essence towards which he projects himself, which he hopes to reach in the future, not by rational planning, but by inner subjective development.[138]

In this statement we find the same principles that made Read turn to political anarchism in the first place, and he acknowledged that political freedom necessarily required a philosophy of freedom, such as idealism or existentialism.

---

138 Herbert Read, 'Existentialism, Marxism and Anarchism', reproduced in Herbert Read, *Anarchy and Order* (London: Faber and Faber, 1954) 148

All of this was indicative of Read's desire to establish a coherent intellectual system in the immediate post-Second Word War period and a belief that this should encompass not only his philosophical but his political views. It was a deliberate and self-conscious programme undertaken to challenge the intellectual coherency of Marxism.[139] What it also demonstrated was the degree to which Read was happy to consider existentialism as simply a manifestation of his understanding of romantic idealism rather than a distinct approach to philosophy in its own right. Existentialism shared deep roots with Read's own philosophy, he noted in the book *The Forms of Things Unknown,* and he found 'much support' for his ideas among contemporary existentialist philosophers.[140]

Yet there were subtle differences that separated Read from existentialism and which made him wary of calling himself an existentialist. In the 1950s existentialism was generally seen

---

139 *Ibid,* 157-8

140 Herbert Read, *Forms of Things Unknown* (London: Faber and Faber, 1960) 28

as an anti-materialist ideology, not unlike certain forms of idealism, denying the actuality of the material world in favour of purely mental creation of reality. Although Read came close to this position, his philosophical outlook was, as he stated again in *The Forms of Things Unknown,* derived from sources other than the writings of existentialist thinkers, including the decidedly materialist phenomenon of art.[141] The primacy Read gave to material and bodily existence is important, not least because the physical nature of art made it difficult to take seriously an ontology of art that neglected material and bodily existence. In a lecture delivered at the Conway Hall in London in 1951, entitled 'Art and the Evolution of Man', Read made clear his belief that the material, physical and tactile properties of art were essential not only to the nature of art itself, but for the function of art in human society.[142]

---

141 *Ibid.*

142 This was subsequently published as Herbert Read, Art and the Evolution of Man (London: Freedom Press, 1951), and then republished again as Herbert Read, 'Art and the Evolution of Man', reproduced in Herbert Read *A One Man Manifesto,* edited by David Goodway (London: Freedom Press, 1994). In this latter edition see in particular page 168.

Yet Read's understanding of existentialism was on this point somewhat mistaken. Although Sartre did occasionally sound like an extreme idealist, for whom things do not exist 'except through consciousness', existentialism did not in general deny the actuality of the material world[143] Sartre was himself a materialist who claimed his philosophy, 'is a materialism and that it gives due weight to both matter and consciousness'.[144] Consequently Sartre's concept of human beings as 'free agents' was not really like Berkeley's situation of reality purely as *idea* in the human mind.[145] Rather it was a notion that individuals were: 'profoundly and inescapably situated in specific social and material conditions.'[146] Had he recognised this perhaps Read would have been willing to adopt existentialism as a definition of his philosophical outlook.

---

143 Hazel Barnes, 'Sartre's Ontology', in Christina Howells (ed.), *The Cambridge Companion to Sartre* (Cambridge: Cambridge University Press, 1992) 24

144 *Ibid*, 17

145 *Ibid*, 25

146 Christina Howells 'Sartre, Jean-Paul', in Edward Craig (ed.), *Routledge Encyclopaedia of Philosophy* (London: Routledge, 1998) 477

As this suggests, despite his very early recognition of existentialism, and his sympathy for its ideas, Read shared with the mainstream English speaking world a belief that the existentialists rejected or were disinterested in the world around them. Read explained this difference in a parable in which he suggested the anti-materialism of the existentialists could be seen in their response to the epistemic trauma of modernity. Read suggested that like all humanity the existentialists stood on the edge of an abyss facing the truth of their own insignificance. Whereas most of humanity was oblivious of the abyss, the existentialists recognised their situation and were overwhelmed by *Angst*. But for Read there was not a simple choice between ignorance of the abyss and *Angst*-ridden knowledge of it. As with his attempt to unify classicism and romanticism, Read synthesised a third response. He suggested that standing at the edge of the abyss was another group of people who saw their true situation as well as any existentialist. But instead of being overwhelmed by *Angst* this group possessed a fascination with both the interior mental world and the exterior material world of apparent existence. According to Read, such people were like Aristotle, and were filled with interest, excitement and wonder. Read suggested that the Aristotelian saw:

> Fire and Air, and Earth and Water, elementary qualities giving birth to all sorts of contrarieties – hot-cold, dry-moist, heavy-light, hard-soft, viscous-brittle, rough-smooth, coarse-fine – sees these combining and interacting and producing worlds and life upon these worlds, and he is lost in wonder.

The litany of simultaneous contrasts is significant here.[147] It resembles Read's contrast and reconciliation of romanticism and classicism, but extends across a range of phenomena. And like the reconciling image provided by art, Read suggested that

147 It is worth comparing this contrast of forms, hard-soft, heavy-light, and so on, with the writing of Read's friend and contemporary Adrian Stokes. For example, Adrian Stokes, *Smooth and Rough* (Faber, 1951).

reading Aristotle might also be 'an antidote' to existentialist *Angst* by returning us to the wonder of the material world.[148]

ACT WISELY NOW

Although Read refused to be labelled an existentialist, existentialism is still useful for understanding Read's extraordinary intellectual affiliations, and for the moral compass it gave his understanding of idealist philosophers. What Read gained from existentialism was not in the end an alternative way of conceptualising reality to that provided by idealists, but an ethical message that the transformation of society depended on an absolute individuality based on absolute responsibility for one's own actions. In this the link with anarchist concepts of freedom was also apparent. Genuine freedom also brought with it genuine responsibility. For Read Sartre's message was that: 'the

---

148 Herbert Read '*Existentialism, Marxism and Anarchism*', reproduced in Herbert Read, *Anarchy and Order* (London: Faber and Faber, 1954) 152-3

slightest human act must be construed as emanating from the future'.[149] This gave everyone a responsibility for whatever future reality might come into being, and in so doing existentialism gave idealism a moral bearing. This was necessary for Read in a post-humanist world in which there was no God to give laws and commandments, and no *a priori* right or wrong. Instead there was a responsibility that extended across art, politics and social relations to avoid acting in what Sartre called 'bad faith'. Bad faith was a denial of responsibility and the denial or responsibility was a denial of individual freedom.[150]

It is easy to see why Read was drawn to this way of thinking. Bad faith is a concept and a phrase that is almost Ruskinian in its moral overtones. In essence if there was to be a kind of new paradise, akin to Eden no less, in which Fourier's anti-tigers might roam and the sea would taste of lemonade, everyone had to take moral responsibility for it coming into

149 Herbert Read, *The Philosophy of Modern Art* (London: Faber and Faber, 1952) 46-7

150 Read's essay 'The Problem of Pornography' explores this theme directly. See Herbert Read, *To Hell with Culture* (London: Routledge, 1963: 2002 reprint) 167 and *passim*

being, or accept moral responsibility for doing nothing to facilitate its coming into being.

THE WONDER OF YOU

In *Existentialism, Marxism and Anarchism* Read's specific description of the Aristotle-like man was as someone who reacted to the world with: 'feelings of profound interest, excitement, wonder'.[151] Wonder is not a phrase one would readily associate with what was effectively a political tract. Wonder suggests pleasure or playfulness and not the serious matter of alienation and epistemic trauma. In the same essay, in a broadside against the Marxist critique of culture and society, Read also suggested that it was probably the failure to acknowledge the place play had in the development of human culture that was the problem with Marxism. 'Perhaps it is this

---

151 Herbert Read '*Existentialism, Marxism and Anarchism*', reproduced in Herbert Read, *Anarchy and Order* (London: Faber and Faber, 1954) 152-3

theory of all work and no play', Read suggested, 'that has made the Marxist such a very dull boy'.[152]

We have to be careful here. As an advocate for creative freedom in the education of children, it is tempting to suggest Read was an exponent of a kind of play-theory of art, known at the time he was writing as the 'play hypothesis'. The play hypothesis suggested art was the byproduct of play, but for Read, while the artist might play with paint, or paper, or wood, or stone, and the poet might play with words or metrical structure, play could not account for the development and purpose of art.[153] The closest he was willing to give a meaningful place to play in the development of art was in quoting Friedrich Schiller's statement that: 'the creation of

152 *Ibid*, 151-2

153 The view that play occurs only in animals that have sufficient economic surplus to spend superfluous energy on pleasure goes back into the writings of Arthur Schopenhauer, Friedrich Schiller and Herbert Spencer in the eighteenth and nineteenth centuries. Contemporary with Read writing after the Second world War the idea was put forward by Johan Huizinga in his book *Homo Ludens: A Study of the Play-Element in Culture,* published by Routledge, when Read was a Director of the firm, in 1949. Herbert Read's critique appears in Herbert Read, 'Art and the Evolution of Consciousness', in *The Journal of Aesthetics and Art Criticism,* vol. 13, no. 2, December 1954, 145f

something new is not accomplished by the intellect, but by the play instinct, from some inner necessity.'[154]

As this suggests, art was, for Read, too important to be considered a byproduct of play, or indeed a byproduct of anything else. For Read art was, as Frank Kermode noted in his review of Read's book *The Tenth Muse,* 'a formative, not a rhetorical activity.'[155] Art was a method to achieve radically new relationships that might in turn lead to radically new realities. This radical method was at the heart of Read's theorising as an invocation of a primary, and ultimately biologically-predetermined, human need to constantly renegotiate our relationship with the external world. Stressing this, Read stated unambiguously that: 'Art is a biological function.'[156] Through art humankind fulfilled a biological and functional necessity on which the survival of the human species depended, namely the

154 Herbert Read, 'Originality', in the *The Sewanee Review,* vol. 61, no. 4, Autumn, 1953, 549

155 Frank Kermode, 'Review of Herbert Read's *The Tenth Muse,* in *The Review of English Studies,* vol. 10, no. 40 (new series), November, 1959, 434

156 Herbert Read, 'The Disintegration of Form in Modern Art', in *Studio International,* vol.169, no.864, April 1965, 144

reconciliation of the internal desire for psychological comfort, placed on humanity by the evolution of consciousness, with the external flux of an ever changing and often threatening world in which we must live. If playfulness had any role in this functional process it was simply to provide the raw material for the dialectical interplay, bringing together disparate elements that might seem almost ridiculous in their incongruity. As the Surrealists suggested, those elements might seem as comic as: 'the chance meeting of a sewing machine and an umbrella on a dissecting table'.[157]

A SURREAL MEETING OF MINDS

If Read's attitude to play was ambiguous, certainly the playful interaction of incongruous opposites seen in Surrealism was important. In 1936 Read wrote:

157 Isidore-Lucien Ducasse, quoted in J.H. Matthew, *Introduction To Surrealism* (Pennsylvania State University Press, Pennsylvania, 1965) 105

In dialectical terms we claim that there is a continual state of opposition between the world of objective fact – the sensational and social world of active and economic existence – and the world of subjective fantasy. This opposition creates a state of disquietude, a lack of spiritual equilibrium, which it is the business of the artist to resolve. He resolves the contradiction by creating a synthesis, a work of art, which combines elements from both these worlds, eliminates others, but which for the moment gives us a qualitatively new experience.[158]

With this in mind it is apparent that in Read's thinking there were perhaps few more profoundly strange meetings on a metaphorical dissecting table than that of John Ruskin and Friedrich Nietzsche. Yet it was precisely through an unlikely synthetic interplay of Ruskin and Nietzsche's ideas that Read

158 Herbert Read, 'Introduction' to Herbert Read (ed), *Surrealism* (London: Faber and Faber, 1936) 40

brought the Victorian patrician and the scourge of the Wilhelmian bourgeoisie together as companions, the product of which formed the bedrock of his beliefs.

Read first encountered Ruskin's work around 1910,[159] and his admiration was reinforced shortly afterwards at meetings of the Leeds Arts Club where Ruskin, along with Nietzsche, was held in extremely high regard.[160] Ruskin was associated with the neo-Gothic movement, a fact Read noted himself in one of the few passages where he felt able to praise the Gothic Revival.[161] Ironically, although Read was an arch-modernist, the similarities between his ideas and those of Ruskin can lead one to characterise Read not simply as a modernist, but as the last Gothic revivalist, an idea that already

159 Herbert Read, *The Contrary Experience* (London: Faber and Faber, 1963) 273

160 See David Thistlewood, *Formlessness and Form* (London: Routledge, 1984) 30

161 Herbert Read, *The Contrary Experience* (London: Faber and Faber, 1963) 276

hints at a new hybrid coming into existence through Readian dialectical thinking.[162]

Like Hulme in the early twentieth century, Ruskin characterised art in terms of a binary system based on the romanticism versus classicism debate, although in Ruskin's schema the opposites were seen often in architectural terms as an opposition of gothic and classical building styles. What is significant here is that for Ruskin such architectural styles were not simply question of fashion or taste, they carried ethical meaning. Despite this it is rare, even in recent studies, to find comment on the dialectical implications of this aspect of Ruskin's work. Although the classical and the gothic in architecture were Ruskin's most familiar opposites, the principle of dialectical thinking this set up in his mind was expanded by

162 I am grateful to Lee Beard for his paper and comments that suggested the origins of Read's theory of abstraction lay in his study of ceramics whilst a curator at the Victoria and Albert Museum, in London. In these a suggestion was made for a link between Read and the Arts and Crafts movement, one of the last overt manifestations of the Gothic Revival. Lee Beard '"Art without content": Herbert Read, pottery and the non-figurative', paper presented at the *Herbert Read Conference*, Tate Britain, London, June 2004. It is also notable to consider Read's self-acknowledged romanticism in the light of Henry Beers's statement in 1902 that romanticism was also a form of mediæval revivalism, which Beers claimed was commonly accepted. See Henry Beers, *A History of English Romanticism in the Nineteenth Century* (London: Kegan Paul, 1902) v-vi. Read also had an early interest in Guild Socialism, a political manifestation of late nineteenth-century mediaeval revivalism, associated with William Morris.

him to include other apparent opposites, much as we see in Read. In *Modern Painters* Ruskin advised art students to: 'go to Nature in all singleness of heart, and walk with her laboriously and trustingly, having no other thought but how to best penetrate her meaning and instruction, and remember the instruction; rejecting nothing, selecting nothing and scorning nothing'. While for many this has appeared to justify a mimetic or realist reproduction of nature in art, the statement carried with it an important rider which linked Ruskin's attitude closely to the dialectics of Read. By studying nature in a mimetic way the art student was only undertaking part of the creative process. Ruskin also advised the student to become imaginative and poetic. '[W]hen their memories are stored, and their imagination fed, and their hands firm,' Ruskin stated, 'let them take up the scarlet and gold, give the reins to their fancy, and show us what their heads are made of.'[163]

---

163 John Ruskin, *Modern Painters,* vol. 1, part 2 (London: Smith, Elder and Co, 1843) 416-7

The same point was made by Ruskin in his lecture *Sesame and Lillies* where he suggested that alongside the simple reproduction of nature in art there must also be: 'the visible operation of human intellect in the presentation of truth'.[164]

Clearly Ruskin did not see art as a straightforward reproduction of nature, but as a dialectical process that brought together the mind and nature, the classical and the romantic, or in Ruskin's terminology the classical and the gothic.[165] This was not an inevitable position for him to reach, and it arose only after Ruskin had experienced his own epistemic trauma later in life, and became disillusioned with Christianity. Only then was he able to discard the definitive notion of truth found in Christian humanism and make the unashamedly dialectical statement that: 'nature is nobly animal [and] nobly spiritual –

164 Delivered at the South Kensington Museum, London, in January 1858.John Ruskin, *Sesame and Lilies* (London: Collins and Co, 1865; 1907 reprint) 110

165 The classical and the gothic was also Wilhelm Worringer's formulation of this division in the first quarter of the twentieth century.

coherently and irrevocably so; neither part of it may, but at its peril, expel, despise, or defy the other'.[166]

In this we see how Ruskin's aesthetic came close to Read's understanding of romantic idealism, with creativity the result of the encounter of opposites. In Ruskin's case those opposites were the advocacy of truth to nature on one side, and the poetic imagination on the other which he summarised with the terms *mimesis* and *poesis*. Translated to Read the former represented classical knowledge, or the outscape, the latter romantic intuition, or the inscape. Ruskin even used a Readian sounding term to describe the product of this dialectic, calling it *vital*.[167]

Nietzsche also hypothesised two opposite tendencies, a kind of *mimesis* and *poesis*, but he labelled these the Apollonian and the Dionysian. Like Ruskin, there was a need in Nietzsche's

---

166 John Ruskin, *Modern Painters,* vol. 5, part 7 (London: Smith, Elder and Co, 1860) 264

167 John Ruskin 'The Schools of Art in Florence', reproduced in John Ruskin, *The Complete Works of John Ruskin,* vol. 23 (London: George Allen, 1906) 211. Ruskin used the work *vitalistic* in many places. For example John Ruskin, *The Seven Lamps of Architecture,* quoted in John Ruskin *The Lamp of Beauty,* edited by Joan Evans (Oxford: Phaidon, 1959) 198. Specifically for a definition of 'living art' which is close to Read's definition of vitality see page 201.

thinking for these to be reconciled. But as Read recognised, Nietzsche's theory of reconciliation was problematic as Nietzsche did not appear to consider Apollo and Dionysos to be of equal worth. Instead Nietzsche seemed to suggest the Dionysian was prioritised as the vital element in life while the Apollonian took on the aspect of a dull ordering principle. In effect, Dionysos appeared a wild and free child, while Apollo seemed little more than a stern and disapproving governess. To be fully useful to Read what was needed was a Nietzschean dialectic of equal opposites which could create a balanced – Read used the Aristotelian word 'measured' – synthesis.[168] This recasting of Nietzsche was not difficult for him to find. In part it came through the example of Ruskin, but it also came from the writings of another admirer of both Ruskin and Nietzsche, Alfred Orage. For Orage the Dionysian and Apollonian principles set out by Nietzsche did not seem to be so uneven. Read developed a close friendship with Orage whilst writing for

168 Herbert Read, *Icon and Idea* (London: Faber and Faber, 1955) 51

Orage's weekly journal *The New Age* in the 1920s, a time when, Read later admitted, he 'worshipped' Orage.[169] In his 1906 book *Friedrich Nietzsche: The Dionysian Spirit of the Age*,[170] Orage presented the opposition of Nietzsche's Apollo and Dionysos in terms far more balanced than Nietzsche himself ever did:

> Apollo and Dionysos may stand respectively for law and liberty, duty and love, custom and change, science and intuition, art and inspiration: in their larger aspects they are symbols of oppositions that penetrate the very stuff of consciousness and life; they are its warp and woof. Thus Apollo stands for Form as against Dionysos for Life; for Matter as against Energy; for the Human as against the Superhuman. Apollo is always on the side of the formed, the definite, the restrained, the rational; but

169 Quoted in James King, *Herbert Read: The Last Modern* (London: Weidenfeld and Nicolson, 1990) 71

170 Read's copy of this is now in the University of Leeds Brotherton Library, Special Collections. Alfred Orage, *Nietzsche: The Dionysian Spirit of the Age* (London: T.N. Foulis, 1906), The book has been republished as Alfred Orage, *Friedrich Nietzsche: The Dionysian Spirit of the Age* (London: Orage Press, 2014)

Dionysos is the power that destroys forms, that leads the definite into the infinite, the unrestrained, the tumultuous and passionate.

In fairness, Nietzsche also wrote on the reconciliation of these unequal forces, notably in *The Birth of Tragedy,* but in Orage there was the far more unambiguous suggestion that neither Dionysos nor Apollo was pre-eminent: 'Dionysos without Apollo would be unmanifest, pure energy', Orage wrote. 'Apollo without Dionysos would be dead, inert'.[171]

Although the idea of classicism and romanticism (under whatever names) being reconciled became part of the general *Zeitgeist* by the 1920s, as evidenced by Herford and Read himself, the early date of 1906 at which Orage embraced the idea, and recast Nietzsche in light of it, is significant. It would be at least another decade before Bergson's not dissimilar attempts at dialectical reconciliation would become widely

171 Alfred Orage, *Nietzsche: The Dionysian Spirit of the Age* (Mitcham: Orage Press, 2014) 34-5

known in Britain,[172] and so it is probably fair to say that Orage's presentation of Nietzsche effectively primed Read to accept the synthesist dialectical propositions he discovered later in writers such as Coleridge, Schelling, Worringer and Jung.

In terms of Ruskin and Nietzsche it was not only Orage and Read who recognised the curious connections between them, even if it has been largely neglected and rejected by later commentators.[173] Georg Simmel saw it as early as 1903.[174] In their concern with the reconciliation of oppositional forces into

172 For example, the first Bergson text to be translated into English was in 1910 with F.L. Pogson's translation of *Time and Free Will* (London: Allen and Unwin, 1910). Although translations of his books flowed quickly after this it was really anti-German feeling in the First World War, some of it promulgated by Bergson himself, that dislodged Nietzsche from being the philosopher of choice for much of the cultural avant-garde. In terms of the argument I am putting forward here the most relevant Bergson text is Henri Bergson, *Matter and Memory,* translated by Nancy Margaret Paul and W. Scott Palmer (London: George Allen and Unwin 1911). The most relevant chapter in this book is chapter 1, originally entitled "'Of the Selection of Images for Conscious Presentation: What Our Body Means and Does'" was republished in Sunil Manghani, Arthur Piper and Jon Simons (eds.), *Images: A Reader* (London: Sage, 2006).

173 For example see Edward Skidelsky, 'England's Doubt' in *Prospect Magazine,* July 1999. Skidelsky, commenting on the 'death of God' in the nineteenth century, accepted figures such as Ruskin, George Eliot, Hardy, Arnold and Carlyle in this role, but bemoaned that they were not like their mainland European counterparts: 'Where, among the dreary congregation at God's funeral [in England], are the "lost violent souls": the de Sades, the Bakunins, the Nietzsches? Do even our atheists have to be respectable?' A notable and fascinating exception to the neglect of this seemingly unlikely connection is provided by Jeremy Tambling, 'Interrupted Traffic: Reading Ruskin', in *The Modern Language Review,* vol. 105, no. 1, January 2010, 63f

174 See Georg Simmel, 'Die Grossstadt. Vorträge und Aufsätze zur Städteausstellung', in *Jahrbuch der Gehe-Stiftung Dresden,* vol. 9, 1903, 185-206

a new artistic synthesis, Read found in Ruskin and Nietzsche additional justification for his belief that dialectical reconciliation could be an all encompassing critical, philosophical and political position..

CONCLUSION

In art schools a principle in all good teaching is to encourage students to understand the concept of balance. Balance is not symmetry, although symmetry can be a part of balance. Balance is more like Read's concept of dialectical integration. It is the combination of oppositional forces into a workable, or integrated, whole. In Nietzschean terms we see this in relation to the 'classical' Apollo being brought into a workable relationship with the 'romantic' Dionysos. The Apollonian is safe, predictable and maybe even symmetrical, but also a little dull and uninspiring. The Dionysian is dangerous, unpredictable and asymmetrical, but also exciting and original. Apollo and Dionysos are nice ancient gods to hang this idea on to, the puritan Apollo set against the drunkard Dionysos, but the point was clear for Read: one without the other was deeply problematic.

As we have seen, Read used the Aristotelian term 'measured' to describe the balancing of oppositional forces, but another term used in art studio teaching to describe the same unity of opposites is *tension*. This is where Read's theory of art and poetics becomes highly practical, and why he has been such a popular a figure amongst artists and art students. To talk about opposites coming together and being integrated into a new unity is to talk about the basic process of art. On a canvas a simple form like a square set in the centre of the picture plane is perhaps too predictable and dull, or we might say too ordered and classical, and too Apollonian. So we might move it a little to the left, or turn it a few degrees on its axis, or lop off a corner, or add some additional line for form to disrupt its predictability. In so doing we bring romantic Dionysos into the equation. This might seem too simple a way to describe the act of making art, but multiply this simple act a thousand or tens of thousands of times when dealing with a complex work of art, and you have the Readian principle of art in action, and in a highly practical way. The known and predictable which gives us psychological comfort is disrupted by the unknown and unexpected, a process as much in evidence in Titian as it is in Matisse. The aim with this is never to allow the Dionyisan or romantic principle absolute free reign, as that would lead to traumatic chaos: but the presence of the romantic principle is necessary to maintain the *vitality* that the Apollonian or classical principle alone lacks, namely the creative possibility of a more satisfying answer to the issue posed by Ruskin as the problem of art: the quest for truth. As Read suggested in his evocatively titled book *Art and Alienation* this is a quest that probably has no end and no definitive answer, only a never ending task of undertaking the quest for truth.[175]

That Read believed tension in art was not simply a matter of decorative pictorial composition is significant. It was related to human happiness in a profound way, making a link between art and society that goes way beyond façile attempts to turn art into socially-relevant political illustration. Art provided a metaphor for the balance that was needed between the romantic inner self and the classical outer world, a balance that had been destroyed by the painful epistemic trauma of modernity. But art was not only a metaphor for Read. It was a method and a process to rebalance the inner and outer that is necessary for human health, and this gave art its purpose in human society.

Few writers on art have ever given artists a more important role in life, not as mere decorators or social commentators, but as facilitators of human happiness. The role

175 Herbert Read, *Art and Alienation* (New York: Viking, 1969) 68

of romantic idealism and anarchism in this is key. Unless one has a theory of the capacity of humankind to change reality, rather than simply live it, then happiness is no more than an arbitrary byproduct of life which the lucky few amongst us may possess. Even if the result of Read's philosophy of art is that we are given a potentially unrealisable quest, then the truth about Read is that he stills gives us a theory of empowerment and hope in place of a dogma of futility and despair. But more than this he gives us a methodology which has at its heart both art and the artist. The artist might be like Don Quixote, forever tilting at windmills 'in fierce and unequal combat' in a vain attempt to force them to give up their true nature as 'monstrous giants', but without the Quixotic artist life is robbed of glory.[176]

Shortly before his death in 1968, in an interview for the journal *Art Education,* Read summed up his position on art:

---

176 Read had a great deal to say on both glory and Cervantes. See Herbert Read, *The Sense of Glory* (Cambridge: Cambridge University Press, 1929) *passim*

It is a method by means of which the individual seeks a harmonious relationship with society and his own environment. It is, in a way, the answer to alienation and it is the achievement of a serene relationship with other people and with one's environment.[177]

177 Foster Wygant, 'A Conversation with Herbert Read', in *Art Education,* vol. 20, no. 9, December 1967, 33

Further Reading

- Egbert, Donald Drew, *Social Radicalism and the Arts* (New York: Alfred J Knopf, 1970)
- Getsy, David (ed), *Sculpture and the Pursuit of the Modern Ideal in Britain, c1880-1930* (Aldershot: Ashgate, 2004)
- Goodway, David, *Herbert Read Reassessed* (Liverpool: Liverpool University Press, 1998)
- Green, Christopher (ed), *Art Made Modern: Roger Fry's Vision of Art* (London: Merrell Holberton, 1999)
- Harding, Jason, *The Criterion: Cultural Politics and Periodical Networks in Inter-War Britain* (New York and Harrison Charles, *English Art and Modernism* (London: Allen Lane, 1981)
- King, James, *The Last Modern* (London: Weidenfeld and Nicolson, 1990)
- Martin, Wallace, *Orage as Critic* (London: Routledge, 1974)
- Massey, Anne, *The Independent Group* (Manchester: Manchester University Press 1995)
- Mook, Delo and Vargish, Thomas, *Inside Modernism* (New Haven and London: Yale University Press, 1999)
- Morris, Lynda and Radford, Robert, *AIA: The Story of the Artists' International Association 1933-1953* (Oxford: Museum of Modern Art, 1983)
- Murray, Chris, *Key Writers on Art: The Twentieth Century* (London and New York: Routledge, 2003)
- Orage, Alfred, *Nietzsche: The Dionysian Spirit of the Age* (Mitcham: Orage Press, 2014)
- Paraskos, Michael (ed), *Re-Reading Read: New Views on Herbert Read* (London: Freedom Press, 2007)
- Paraskos, Stass (ed), *Homage to Herbert Read,* exh, cat (Canterbury: Canterbury College of Art, 1984)
- Peters Corbett, David, *The Modernity of English Art* (Manchester: Manchester University Press, 1997)
- Read, Benedict and Thistlewood, David, *Herbert Read: A British Vision of World Art* (London: Lund Humphries, 1993)
- Remy, Michel, *Surrealism in Britain* (London: Lund Humphries, 2001)
- Saler, Michael, *The Avant-Garde in Interwar England* (New York and Oxford: Oxford University Press, 1999)
- Sinfield, Alan, *Literature, Politics and Culture in Postwar Britain* (London: Athlone, 1997)
- Steele, Tom, *Alfred Orage and the Leeds Arts Club 1893-1923* (Mitcham: Orage Press, 2009)
- Thistlewood, David (ed), *Barbara Hepworth Reconsidered* (Liverpool: Liverpool University Press, 1996)
- Thistlewood, David, *Herbert Read: Formlessness and Form* (London: Routledge, 1984)

- Treece, Henry (ed), *Herbert Read: An Introduction to His Work by Various Hands* (London: Faber and Faber, 1944)
- Woodcock, George, *Herbert Read: The Stream and the Source* (London: Faber and Faber, 1972)

Select List of Books by Herbert Read

- *A Coat of Many Colours* (London: Faber and Faber, 1947)
- *A Concise History of Modern Painting* (London: Thames and Hudson, 1964)
- *Æsthetic Judgement and the Archetype* (Padua: Edizioni della Rivista di Estetica, 1958)
- *A One-Man Manifesto* (London: Freedom Press, 1994)
- *A World Within a War* (London: Faber and Faber, 1944)
- *Anarchy and Order* (London: Faber and Faber, 1954)
- *Annals of Innocence and Experience* (London: Faber and Faber, 1940)
- *Art and Alienation* (New York: Viking, 1970)
- *Art and Society* (London: William Heinemann, 1937)
- *Art Now* (London: Faber and Faber, 1933)
- *Art Now* (London: Faber and Faber, 1936)
- *English Prose Style* (London: Bell, 1928)
- *Essays in Literary Criticism* (London: Faber and Faber, 1969)
- *Essential Communism* (London: Stanley Nott, 1935)
- *Existentialism, Marxism and Anarchism* (London: Freedom Press, 1949)
- *Form in Modern Poetry* (London: Faber and Faber, 1932)
- *Forms of Things Unknown* (London: Faber and Faber, 1960)
- *Henry Moore* (London: Thames and Hudson, 1965)
- *Henry Moore: An Appreciation* (London: Zwemmer, 1934)
- *Icon and Idea* (London: Faber and Faber, 1955)
- *In Retreat* (London: Hogarth Press, 1925)
- *Julien Benda and the New Humanism* (Seattle: University of Washington, 1930)

- *Moon's Farm and Other Poems* (London: Faber and Faber, 1955)
- *Naked Warriors* (London: Art and Letters, 1919)
- *Philosophy of Anarchism* (London: Freedon Press, 1940)
- *Poetry and Anarchism* (London: Faber and Faber, 1938)
- *Selected Poetry* (London: Faber and Faber, 1960)
- *Staffordshire Pottery Figures* (London: Duckworth, 1929)
- *Surrealism* (London: Faber and Faber, 1936)
- *The Art of Sculpture* (New York: Bollingen Foundation, 1956)
- *The Contrary Experience* (London: Faber and Faber, 1963)
- *The Cult of Sincerity* (London: Faber and Faber, 1968)
- *The English Vision* (London: Routledge, 1933)
- *The Grass Roots of Art* (New York: Wittenborn, 1946; 1955 reprint)
- *The Green Child* (London: William Heineman, 1935; 1989 reprint)
- *The Innocent Eye* (London: Faber and Faber, 1933; reprint Otley, Smith Settle, 1996)
- *The Meaning of Art* (London: Faber and Faber, 1931)
- *The Philosophy of Modern Art* (London: Faber and Faber, 1952)
- *The Politics of the Unpolitical* (London: Routledge, 1943)
- *The Tenth Muse* (London: Faber and Faber, 1957)
- *The True Voice of Feeling* (London: Faber and Faber, 1953)
- *To Hell with Culture and Other Essays* (London: Routledge, 1963)
- (ed), *Unit One: The Modern Movement in English Architecture, Painting and Sculpture* (London: Cassell, 1934)
- *William Wordsworth* (London: Jonathan Cape, 1930)

Other titles available from
The Orage Press

Between the Riccall and the Rye
Yorkshire writings by Herbert Read
edited by Michael Paraskos and Benedict Read

In this collection of writings we hear Read telling in a straightforward but moving way his memories of a Yorkshire childhood. Through his poetry and prose we gain a real sense of his longing to return. And once he is back in the Ryedale landscape where he was born there is a profound feeling in his writings of him belonging to the land.

ISBN: 978-0956580214

Friedrich Nietzsche:
The Dionysian Spirit of the Age
by Alfred Orage
with a new introduction by Michael Paraskos

Alfred Orage was one of the most significant figures in the modernist art and literary world of early twentieth century Britain. As co-founder of the Leeds Arts Club in 1903 he helped to introduce European modernism to Britain.

Nietzsche was central to Orage's thinking, and in this little book he sought to introduce the German philosopher to a sometimes skeptical British public.

ISBN: 978-0956580252